MW00575928

"Why Isn't My Daughter Married?"

"Why Isn't My Daughter Married?"

Daughters Tell Mothers

The Real Reasons

They're Single

By Patricia Curtis

PRICE STERN SLOAN
Los Angeles

Library of Congress Cataloging-in-Publication Data

Curtis, Patricia, 1929-
"Why isn't my daughter married?"

Bibliography: p.
Includes index.
1. Single women—United States—Psychology.
2. Single women—United States—Attitudes.
3. Mothers and daughters—United States
I. Craig, Patricia, Ph.D. II. Title.
HQ800.2.C87 1988 305.4'890652 87-35732
ISBN 0-89586-585-8

Published by
Price Stern Sloan, Inc.
360 North La Cienega Boulevard
Los Angeles, California 90048

Manufactured in the United States of America

10 9 8 7 6 5 4 3 2 1

Acknowledgments

The authors acknowledge with deep appreciation the participation of the following people in the preparation of this book: Jennie Allen, Sharon Bryant, Lynn Brown, An-Me Chung, Delvia Hart Fischer, Susan Genne, Carla Glasser, Dr. Janet Hall, Janet Hartman, Marcia Hearst, Susan Kelley, Sam Mitnick, Angela Marie Morton, Paul Pierson, Jane Pinkerton, Sherry Warren, and Laura Weide.

Contents

To protect the confidential nature of the survey for this book, the names, professions, and cities of residence of the women who participated have been changed.

Introduction

by

Patricia

Craig

I imagine that it is a rare single woman in this country who is unaware that her marital status has lately been the subject of profound public scrutiny and media attention. For two years now, the marriage prospects of well-educated women, based on the projections of an academic research project dubbed the "Yale-Harvard study," have been the stuff of what cover stories and talk shows are made. As one of the authors of that study, I must confess to a lingering amazement at the amount of coverage it received.

How did it happen? Shortly before Valentine's Day in 1986, a reporter from a local paper in Connecticut called the Sociology Department at Yale in search of a comment on love or marriage appropriate for the holiday. She was referred to Neil Bennett, an Assistant Professor of Sociology, who mentioned that the work he, David Bloom (an associate professor in the Harvard University Economics Department at the time) and I were doing indicated that the marriage rates of relatively well-educated young women had fallen significantly from those of women a generation or so older. Our study also seemed to indicate that some women, rather than postponing marriage, might be forgoing it entirely. The story ran as a short piece on Valentine's Day. But then it got picked up by a wire service and within about a week, the *New York Times* ran a major article on our report. After that, a frenzy of media activity exploded onto lifestyle pages as newspapers, magazines and television shows rushed to do features on single, career-minded women. In retrospect, it seems almost an accident that the results of the study ever became news at all.

For many women, however, the message behind some of the stories was anything but accidental. Rather, pieces with headlines such as "Women Who Tarry May Never Marry," "No M.R.S. for Those Who Wait" or "Single-minded College Girls Put on Shelf at 30" seemed to be a thinly disguised attempt to put ambitious women in their traditional places by warning them that they could not "have it all" and that the price of success in a man's world was personal unhappiness and loneliness. Not surprisingly, women were frustrated and angered by such treatment.

Part of the problem lay, I think, in presenting the results of the study in terms of "chance." To say that a woman of any given age has an *x* percent chance of marrying is a very different statement than to say that *x* percent of all the women of this given age are likely to marry. The first equates getting married with winning a lottery. Marriage becomes something that happens to a woman as if by chance. It implies she has no choice over her life direction and that her future is guided by fate rather than her own decisions.

When looking at the figures from the Yale-Harvard study it is particularly important to remember that individuals should not confuse their own prospects with those of the aggregate group into which they fall. We could not take into account all the different factors that determine a woman's marriageability. Foremost among these, of course, is whether a woman *wants* to marry. Clearly, a woman who desires to get married is more likely to do so than one who does not. Our data, which came from a nationally representative sample of 70,000 women interviewed by the Census Bureau, had no way of telling us what percentage of the unmarried women in the sample had chosen to be single. Thus, we could not know what percentage of single women *who want to marry* will actually do so. Unfortunately, a lot of single women who did want to marry read those statistics and, erroneously, applied them to their own situations.

More fundamentally, though, it seems to me that the popular discussions of the Yale-Harvard study made the assumption that the place of marriage in women's lives has remained unchanged. Those articles blandly ignored the larger social changes that have opened up opportunities for some women to succeed in areas previously closed to them. Traditionally, the role of wife has been more of an all-encompassing one for adult women than the role of husband has been for men. Women have been defined by the places they occupy in the private sphere of the home and family. The image of men is much more dependent on their public roles in work and career. Yet by pitying or chastising the "plight" of single women, many articles failed to recognize that for increasing numbers of women, marriage is not the only means to fulfillment that they have at their disposal.

By this, I don't mean to argue that marriage is now less desired by women than it used to be. It clearly remains at the core of American family life, and the overwhelming majority of young Americans see marriage as something they want and plan to experience. It is simply that we have to consider the possibility that for certain groups of women, especially those who are well-educated, marriage may entail a very different set of propositions than it previously did.

Nowhere is this more evident than with respect to women and employment. As more and more women continue to enter the labor force, it is clear that work has become more central to the lives of women, both single and married, than previously. Young women today probably recognize that they will likely work throughout most of their adult lives. This recognition may lead them to invest in acquiring the education and resources needed for advancement in the job market.

This may certainly lead women to postpone marriage as they opt for more schooling. Plans to work may also have an effect on eventual marriage rates. One sociologist, Andrew Cherlin, in looking at women in their early twenties, found that those who planned to work continuously had a much lower probability of marrying within the next few years than those who did not. This in itself does not mean these women will not marry—indeed, many expected to combine a career with marriage and household responsibilities. However, he noted that as women grow older, they realize how difficult it is to combine careers with childrearing. It is possible that they also even come to see difficulties between having both a career and marriage.

Working also allows women increased financial options. With a relatively high salary, a woman can provide for herself and not feel she has to marry in order to be financially secure. Some researchers recognize this and argue that lower rates of marriage among women with high resources (education, salary, high parental income) might indicate that such women use their resources to "buy out" of marriage. Such women, even if committed in theory to the idea of marriage, won't feel compelled to enter a less than ideal union out of economic necessity.

There is also evidence that women's attitudes about their domestic roles have changed over time and have become much less traditional—especially among those women who work or plan to do so. One study of college women who were career-oriented found that they expected full equality with a partner concerning household responsibilities. Sociologist Karen Mason and her colleagues found that along with education, employment strongly influences women's preferences for less rigid and traditional sex roles at work and within the family.

Changed preferences in favor of egalitarian relationships do not necessarily mean that fewer women will marry. However, if they are unable to find partners who share such a view, some may be induced to forgo marriage. It isn't clear whether women's expectations about equality in relationships have outpaced those of men, but there are some indications that they have.

The college women in one study believed that their own views were fairly non-traditional but also believed that most men did not share such beliefs. Jesse Bernard, a sociologist who has written extensively on women's and men's roles within the family, notes that women have come to expect more emotional sharing and equality from men. Yet, frequently men have not been socialized to offer this and feel at a loss. She argues that the "good provider role" in which a man was supposed to care for his family's material needs has been devalued but that no concomitant role which men are capable of filling has replaced it. Other constraints on equality within a relationship may come from a lack of agreement about what constitutes an equitable division of tasks. Pepper Schwartz and Philip Blumstein's research for *American Couples* found that equality of shared responsibilities was largely fictitious: "Even among couples who profess egalitarian social ideas . . . husbands might say they should share responsibility, [but] when they break it down to time actually spent and chores actually done, the idea of shared responsibility turns out to be a myth."

Other broad social changes have affected the relative attractiveness of marriage. The increased acceptability of cohabitation between unmarried couples means that marriage is less important in legitimating sexual relations. In addition, with available means of birth control, women do not have to marry in order to engage in sexual intimacy. The social stigma attached to being unmarried has also declined. As demographers Arland Thorton and Deborah Freedman point out, the number of people who would be very upset by never marrying has decreased. The same attitude is found among parents when asked how they would feel if their children remained unmarried.

Thus, the issue of why well-educated women may be marrying less than they used to is complex, much more so than many of the popular reports on the subject would lead one to believe. On the one hand, increased options and changing expectations could lead some women away from marriage. On the other, marriage remains a desirable state for most women.

This raises a number of questions about the impact of lower marriage rates that simply cannot be answered by knowing only what those rates are. Ideally, we would like to know whether they are the result of voluntary or involuntary decisions. If women have chosen not to marry, do they see marriage as holding a less central place in their lives than women of previous generations did? Maybe a different scenario is more plausible: Perhaps these women did not consciously choose to be single but have accepted the fact that they are and lead fulfilling lives nonetheless.

Because I find these questions interesting and timely, I agreed to write a survey that would address the issue of singlehood among successful women. The idea to interview their mothers as well was intriguing because it would allow comparisons between different generations of women who had experienced very different life paths. Part of the results of the survey formed the basis of this book, to which the author contributed her own observations, interpretations and conclusions.

The intention of the survey was to interview a variety of single women: those from different areas of the country, of a range of ages and different living situations. In order to find women willing to participate in the survey, I enlisted the help of Jane Pinkerton, the national director of the YWCA. Her enthusiastic support of the project allowed us access to the records of local Y's in Atlanta, Denver, St. Louis, Philadelphia and Portland, Oregon. The target group was women between the ages of 28 and 45 who were never married and had at least a college education—the same women who had been the object of so much media attention.

Invitations to participate in the study were sent, in cases where record keeping was complete, to those women who would fulfill the criteria. In other cases, women of the correct age were asked to participate if they were college educated and had never been married. A cover letter explained only that a survey on single women was being conducted which included a separate questionnaire for their mothers. They also were told that the results of the survey would form the basis of a book. Women who agreed to participate returned an acknowledgment card and sent the names and addresses of their mothers. In addition to this group of women, the author decided to add a number of women she knew from the New York area. In total, 72 women and 58 of their mothers made up the sample.

Questionnaires were sent to the women and their mothers. The women who responded seemed quite eager to be a part of the project. Many commented that they had enjoyed participating and were grateful for being given a voice on this subject. A small number of survey forms were returned by women who did not match the categories that had been asked for—either they had been married or had not completed college—but explained that they knew they weren't quite right but wanted to participate anyway. Unfortunately, their responses had to be excluded. Some women offered to put me in touch with other single women they knew, and most women asked to be informed of the results. It was quite heartening to see women so open and willing to share their feelings about being unmarried despite the often negative publicity that surrounds being single.

After the surveys were returned, the results proved fascinating and suggested new questions. I decided that some issues required a more lengthy forum than short written answers could provide, so in-depth telephone interviews were conducted with about 20 percent of the women and their mothers as a follow-up. The results of these are also discussed in the book.

The findings of the survey are highly suggestive. The reader should keep in mind that they may not apply generally to all single women. A number of limitations must be mentioned. First, this is a small sample and as such could present a distorted picture. Second, the majority of women interviewed are white and of either Protestant or Catholic background (although many claim no current religious affiliation or sentiment). The relative paucity of black and Jewish women means that caution should be exercised in extending conclusions to them since it is possible that cultural differences exist in how they view marriage. Nonetheless, the results are a first step in understanding the concerns of single women and what place they see marriage as holding in their lives.

There is, for example, a powerful indication that the women interviewed have fundamentally different conceptions of marriage than their mothers. At one point in the book, Ms. Curtis mentions that while there is substantial agreement between the women and their mothers on the kinds of qualities each would reject in the women's potential spouse, there are important divergences.

The mothers tend more to reject someone who did not follow the model of men whom women have traditionally married. Women have usually married, or tried to marry, "up," that is, someone who is older, more educated and had a larger income. The mothers in the survey follow this model much more closely than the daughters when ruling out certain characteristics. The mothers were more likely to reject men five years younger than their daughters, those who had a lower level of education and those who earned substantially less. Where the women are more critical than their mothers is on the subjects of sex and politics—two areas where women have often been expected to be deferential to men. That the women overwhelmingly would not accept someone who is sexually unfulfilling and that many of them would not choose to spend a lifetime with someone who had different politics are a demand for a less traditional, more equal partnership.

In another chapter, the author discusses a series of statements with which women were asked how strongly they agreed or disagreed. (See questions **1a** through **1g** in **Appendices A and B**.) Here again, it is striking to notice differences between the women and their mothers. While both groups felt strongly that things other than marriage are important for women, such as success at a career or having friends and an active social life, the mothers indicated very traditional attitudes about how marriage itself should be structured. Mothers were much more insistent than their daughters that women should take their husband's names when they marry, that women should not work outside the home if they have young children and that women should not have children outside of marriage. The mothers seem to be saying that outside of marriage, women can have many options but they see marriage in terms of the experience of their own generation. They emphasize a nuclear family with a traditional division of household labor.

Together, these two sets of results support the notion that single, career-oriented women today demand more equality from marriage than women have in the past. In terms of the themes this book touches on, I think there is a powerful claim that mothers and daughters have different perceptions about marriage which could lead to a lack of shared understanding between them. For the mother who wants her daughter to marry, the message that the she should find a suitable partner may be an impossible demand if mother and daughter have vastly different conceptions of what suitable means.

In broader terms, however, the results suggest that care should be taken when making sweeping statements about marriage. Too often, I think there is the tendency to assume that marriage has an unchanging meaning and function in family life. For some women at least, marriage has come to mean less a source of economic security and the main locus of work than a partnership between equals. Recognizing this means that changes in marriage rates must be looked at in the context of other social changes. For well-educated women, the social forces that have affected their marriage rates have been above all related to their increased opportunities to be self-sufficient and economically independent.

This book presents a picture of women with options, both in terms of careers and marriage. The women are not always content with their situations but they realize and discuss the choices they have made which have lead them there. The addition of their voices and histories to the discussion of women and marriage is important because it allows us to see their singlehood in the context of numerous relationships—those with family, friends, lovers and careers. This removes the entire burden of social change from these women and gives it a clearer and more intelligible perspective.

1

Pressure

''Are you

seeing

anyone?''

"When I was in my early twenties," recalls Sarah, "my mother used to urge me to find a nice Jewish man and marry him. When I entered my thirties and was still unmarried, she dropped the 'Jewish.' And as I approached forty, she dropped 'nice.'"

Sarah is kidding, but the point of her joke will touch a responsive nerve in many women, whatever their background. Whether the "Jewish mother" is real or largely a fiction created by comedians, her character type is apparently recognizable to a great many daughters. In spite of the women's movement and its sizable impact on our attitudes and lifestyles, some things seem to remain unchanged at a fundamental level.

In the last two decades, American society has undergone a series of changes that have profoundly affected our attitudes toward relationships, particularly marriage. During the "me" decade, various forms of self-gratification supplanted more traditional ideas of nurturing and caring for others. A move toward sexual freedom and a relaxed moral code also brought about a decided loss in commitment.

In addition, the women's movement created a conflict between old images of women's roles and the new values of sexual equality. The differing expectations within these shifting roles for women (and for that matter, men) have caused a particular tension between two generations of women—mothers and daughters. Marriage, and everything it implies about women's roles, is at the core of that tension.

Our new social order is replete with ambiguities and inconsistencies that become especially important in the context of a woman's decision to marry or not to marry. The new woman who has forged ahead to take an equal place among men in the workplace cannot count on society for encouragement. She must face the fact that a serious and demanding career will almost inevitably clash with traditional images of her place in society and, perhaps, with her own ideas of personal fulfillment. Having chosen a career, she may be forced repeatedly to review her decision as she faces successive conflicts between her personal life and her work.

Often, it is the mothers of single women who give voice to the contradictions of their dilemma. Many of the same mothers who encouraged careers and independence in their daughters haven't changed in their hearts—they still feel that marriage is essential for a woman's happiness, economic security, and social respectability. As their daughters approach their middle years without mates, these mothers become deeply concerned.

And no matter how hard she tries to hide it, the worried mother of an over-30 unmarried daughter is likely to reveal her concern to her daughter. If the daughter mentions a party she has gone to, the mother may ask with studied casualness: "Did you meet anyone nice?" If her daughter comments about a man she has gone out with, the mother will query, "Are you going to see him again?" And if the daughter has a steady boyfriend, her mother almost certainly wants to know: "When are you two getting married?"

But for a daughter of the new generation, marriage is no longer the simple catch-all solution for happiness. Yet, based on the commentary of those around her, a delay in marrying is viewed with suspicion: Is she too fussy? A man-hater? Unattractive? Gay? Rejecting her "proper" role?

Although many unmarried women have developed a variety of ways of coping with the preoccupation others show in their singlehood, the comments of others are irritating, even painful. Whatever her reason for not marrying, it is a rare woman who can always react with forbearance in the face of that sometimes relentless and always unsolicited concern, whether it be from mother, relatives, friends, or co-workers. Their subtle or overt questions and free opinions about her unmarried state make it difficult for her to keep her sense of self-worth firmly intact. The message seems to be that a woman cannot be complete without a man. Some single women report being made to feel out of step with society. As one expressed it, "This is a very couple-oriented world."

Caroline Bird once argued that American society has at its core a system of values that "keeps women down." Despite the fact that liberal tradition and equal opportunities for education have helped women to rise in society's ranks, in spite of battles won long ago for voting, for legal equality, for the right to hold and trade property, women are inexorably seen in relation to biological roles as childbearers and performers of child-rearing tasks.

Certainly, the images and attitudes connected with childbearing come into play in the highly charged exchanges between mothers and daughters in their discussions of marriage and careers. Even if not squarely stated, the subject of childbearing is certainly part of the hidden agenda revealed in the inflections, if not clearly in the words, of a mother's concern. For these new daughters, the messages that mothers continually give out only exacerbate the questions they are already struggling with in the face of supposed social change.

That Study

Regardless of a general, surface acknowledgment and acceptance of women's enlarged arena of opportunity, there remains a hard core of traditionalism insofar as marriage is concerned. It is not surprising, then, that great numbers of single women reacted strongly to the widely publicized demographic study which predicted that their marital possibilities were slim. The project, conducted by a team of statistical researchers at Harvard and Yale Universities—Neil Bennett, David Bloom, and Patricia Craig—was actually a scholarly analysis of changing marriage patterns over time.

As Craig describes in her introduction to this book, buried within that professional paper and tangential to its main thesis was the mention of declining marriage probabilities for college-educated white women who were born in the United States during the "baby boom" of the mid-1950s. According to the projections, about 80 percent of college-educated white women in general will marry, but those who are unmarried at age 30 have predictably only a 20 percent likelihood of marrying; by age 35, the chances that they will marry drop to 5 percent; only about 2 percent of single 40-year-olds are likely to marry.

This small part of a professional study, intended only for fellow social scientists, instead became a media event. Newspapers and magazines ran with it: "Too Late for Prince Charming?" asked the rather coy headline in one major magazine. Others jeered cleverly: "No M.R.S. Degree for Those Who Wait" and "Women Who Tarry May Never Marry!"

Taken out of context and exploited, the projections of the Harvard/Yale study, or as it came to be known, *that* study, were presented as sounding the death bell for any chances of happiness for most single women over 30. The tone of such articles strongly suggested that by becoming more independent of men, and daring to postpone marriage until established in their careers, women were only getting what they deserved, destined for spinsterhood, with all of the emotional and social handicaps that loaded term implies. The articles seemed to be an attempt to put career-oriented women back in "their place" by scare tactics.

These popular articles failed to examine the actual social, psychological, and demographic conditions that affect the declining marriage rate among women. A year after the Yale/Harvard study was afflicted with so much misleading publicity, the *New York Times* ran a long front-page story entitled "Single Women: Coping with the Void," a title that clearly set the tone. The article was based largely on conversations with no more than 24 single women encountered at singles' gatherings and psychiatrists' offices, augmented by the opinions of a hairdresser whose clients confide in her and a therapist who believes women are single because of neurotic conflicts. The story solemnly presented a most dismal picture of unmarried women's lives.

Whatever a woman's feelings about marrying might be, the media attention given to the Harvard/Yale study nevertheless generated feelings of panic, depression, and anger. A spate of subsequent articles appeared that quoted different statistics and asserted that the Harvard/Yale study was flawed; still, many single women felt betrayed. Those who were already anxious to be married reacted with despair; those who were serenely unconcerned about marriage felt they were being told that they they had missed the boat and that their lives were therefore worthless.

The New Survey

The furor aroused by that study inevitably exacerbated an already existing anxiety among the mothers of many unmarried women. To explore the feelings and attitudes of unmarried women and their mothers, and to ask them to speak about the effect of the daughters' unmarried status on the relationships between them, Patricia Craig formulated a new survey in two parts—one for daughters, one for mothers—especially for this book. This survey was circulated to college-educated single women over 25 years of age in the East, South, Midwest, and West, to get as broad a picture of attitudes as possible. Women who agreed to participate were asked to enlist their mothers in the survey as well.

The questionnaires were sent out and returned individually, to protect the confidential nature of the answers. However, whenever both mothers' and daughters' were returned, it was possible to match them up through a coded system.

The daughters' survey sought to examine several possibilities. Are these single women anxious to marry but are unable to find mates? Or, are they choosing not to marry? Or, would they like to marry but are being very selective? Do they regard marriage as less central to their lives than it was to their mothers? If they do wish to marry, are they having trouble finding men with whom they can envision achieving the kind of partnerships they want? Or, have they accepted singlehood and created lives for themselves that give them happiness and fulfillment?

As for their mothers, is there a gap between their expectations for their daughters, and those of the daughters themselves? Are there social factors today that they are not fully aware of? Are they deeply anxious about their daughters chances for marriage? Even if they see their daughters' lives as not quite fulfilled, are they nevertheless supportive? Or do they believe their daughters can be happy whether they are married or not?

Their answers form the basis for this book. In the survey, unmarried women and their mothers reveal, often in their own words, their feelings, beliefs, and hopes. Undoubtedly, they tell things they could not explain to one another.

The Daughters

Who are the never-married women whose voices will be heard throughout this book? Those who answered the survey range in age from late 20's to early 40's, the majority being in their 30's and representing the peak of the baby boom of the mid-1950s.

All are employed full time. Some also attend school, and over one-third already have advanced degrees. They are attorneys, designers, teachers, nurses, social workers, secretaries, office managers, travel agents, real estate brokers; they are analysts or consultants; they work with computers or in banks; they are on the staffs of public relations or advertising agencies; they own their own businesses. A few are graduate students. Almost all expect to be working continuously for the next 15 years at least.

In terms of their career goals, the women were asked to rate their current status on a scale that ranged from a beginner, at 1, to the highest level, at 7. Most women saw themselves as somewhere in the middle, suggesting that they plan to move ahead in their careers. Some indicated that they would like to remain in the same field but in different jobs. Quite a few hoped to switch careers, go into more creative work or into business for themselves.

The annual incomes of the women in the survey covered a wide range, from $8,000 to $60,000, though a few East Coast women earned more since salaries (and living costs) are higher in eastern cities. Average income was $24,000—with a slightly higher average ($26,000) for women in New York and some other East Coast cities. Not surprisingly, the women with the lowest incomes tended to be younger than the higher-salaried women.

A marked difference between these women and those of previous generations is that the vast majority no longer live at home with their parents. There are some national reports that a number of young people today who normally would be in their own homes are living with parents because of the shortage and high costs of housing. This did not hold true for the vast majority of the women in the survey for this book. They live alone, or with roommates, or with their lovers. A third of them have companion animals—cats or dogs, or both. About a third own their homes or apartments; they not only earn enough to do so but they assume the necessary responsibilities of ownership.

They contrast sharply not only with women of their mothers' generations but with many women who came just before them.

"My generation became adult just a few years before the feminism of the '60s, when women began to think and talk about options and take their careers seriously," says Ellen, who is unmarried and in her late 40's. "We didn't have the advantage of being on the cutting edge of the women's movement. Many of my female contemporaries and I assumed we would work only until we got married. No woman I knew said 'If I get married,' it was 'When I get married' . . . and we treaded water professionally. I was first offered the chance to move into management when I was 30, and I turned it down—something none of my male counterparts would have done, nor would few women today.

"I did break tradition by moving out of my parents' house after college and taking an apartment with another young woman, but even then, we unconsciously behaved as though we were only marking time. In fact, our mind was set such that neither of us spent much money on nice things for the apartment. My roommate had inherited a set of beautiful crystal goblets, which were kept at the back of our kitchen cupboard. It never even occurred to us to use them, not even for a special occasion! They were being saved for when she was married.

"My parents had been deeply ashamed when I left home in the first place; they never visited my apartment, even though they lived in the same city. Whenever I went home for Sunday dinner or whatever, the subject of my living arrangement was never discussed. Later, when I lived for a while with a boyfriend, I never even told them. It would have upset them too much."

Most of the women surveyed for this book come from intact families in middle-class, urban backgrounds. About half feel very or somewhat religious; half feel not very or not at all religious. They are Protestant, Catholic, Jewish, and atheist or agnostic. Ten women indicated that their choice of religion or non-religion was "other," perhaps meaning that they feel or participate in some form of spirituality but are not identified with an organized religion.

One woman has a Master's degree in Divinity, but says most of her class chose ecumenical work outside the church rather than within. She herself indicates that the patriarchal nature of theology became unacceptable to her.

In the matter of religion, the daughters are very different from their mothers, nearly all of whom reported having strong or some religious feelings.

In Their Own Words

It has been fashionable for some time to blame mothers for most of the problems and failures of their offspring. And as jokers often depict them, they are also presumably nags who doggedly urge their adult children, especially their daughters, toward the altar. Whether this is an accurate image of some mothers, or largely an unfair fiction, it strikes a deep chord.

The survey addressed to mothers for this book sought to determine whether they worry about their daughters' possibilities for marriage, what factors—including their own backgrounds—might influence the extent to which they worry, how their concern is manifested, and its effect on their daughters.

Far more than half of the mothers who answered the survey report that they do worry to some degree about their unmarried daughters. But interestingly, many mothers who said that they worry are apparently successful in disguising their anxiety from their daughters. Fewer daughters reported feeling pressured by their mothers than might be imagined, judging by the numbers of mothers who confessed that they do worry.

One explanation might be that some mothers express their concern in ways that the daughters do not perceive as pressure. (Conversely, of course, daughters might interpret certain behavior on the part of their mothers as "pressure" whether the mothers actually intend it or not.)

Many of the women who answered the survey indicated that they do not feel pressured to marry, by their mothers or anyone else. Of those who do, only about half said they feel pressured specifically by their mothers. Pressure comes from others as well. The most common source of pressure mentioned by the daughters was other relatives, followed by mothers, married friends, and co-workers. Fathers and single friends were seen as less of a problem in this regard.

Here, some of the women who reported that they feel pressured describe the ways it is manifested—and their reactions:

"People are always asking me why I'm single," says a 33-year-old Georgia woman. "They initiate long discussions explaining to me what I'm doing wrong." How does this make her feel? "Angry, depressed, resentful, and hopeless," she replies.

Christine, a 32-year-old medical technician, says her mother and father frequently make backhanded comments about her unmarried state. Her married friends don't bother to be subtle, and they sometimes even tease her. While Christine becomes angry at her parents, she tries to keep her cool around others. "Usually I calmly say something to the effect that sure, I'd like to be married some day, but I'm not ready yet, or I haven't found the right person, or whatever I think of at the moment," she reports. "Sometimes I feel really hurt, but I never let anyone see it."

Carol is an instructor at a university. Her mother, father, other relatives, and married friends continually ask her if she's seeing anyone special. If she's not, they want to know if she's making efforts to meet people. "Some of them even have the nerve to ask me what it is I'm doing that turns men off!" states Carol. "My reactions range from annoyance to defensiveness to deep embarrassment."

Emily, a textbook editor, complains that her mother has "started making noises about grandchildren." An aunt takes every opportunity to ask if she is dating, thinking about marriage. Some of her married friends seem to flaunt their married state. "Though I try not to show it, I feel myself becoming hurt and defensive, even hostile," Emily says. "Worse yet, I wonder if perhaps there's something wrong with me—maybe my appearance, or more likely, the way I relate to men. I end up thinking I must be sending off some kind of vibes that keep men away.

"I sometimes wish my mother *had* put pressure on me to marry a long time ago," Emily adds a bit wistfully. "Then I wouldn't be feeling this way now, in my 30's." (Most mothers will recognize this as an example of the classic "damned if you do, damned if you don't" situation that goes with the job.)

Denise is a successful dress designer, and at age 32 feels pressure from all directions. "My mother is always asking questions about my social life, as if every date I have is a prospective husband. She goes out of her way to talk about her friends' children who are getting married, having children. In fact, when I see my own friends getting married and having kids, I feel pressure from myself.

"All this depresses me and makes me wonder if I'm somehow inadequate," Denise continues. "I think society confers a lot of status on married people; this is even reflected in the media. I worry that my family and friends might feel sorry for me. Yet, judging by many of the marriages I see around me, I know I wouldn't want to be in any of them. I have very conflicting emotions."

A woman who is still in her 20's reports: "I have been dating my boyfriend for three years, and consequently I'm hit with a lot of comments and assumptions from my parents, siblings, other relatives, married friends. I usually bristle with annoyance, but then I wonder if I should be getting scared."

Lynn, a 37-year-old public relations executive, does not feel pressured by her mother but by her sister and a colleague. "My sister acts as though I am of little consequence because I haven't done what she did—marry and have children. It's odd, because I don't think she's happily married. Also, she considers herself a committed feminist, a position that's certainly inconsistent with her attitude toward me.

"The man I work with is forever telling me that since I'm so great he can't understand why I'm not married, as if my being great should automatically make me married. He tries to make me say that I'd be happier married; he wants me to confirm what he believes."

How does Lynn react to such pressure? "I used to argue until I realized that most people who pressure me don't really care about me, they're just seeking to validate their own lives and decisions. If they think about me at all, they see me as a threat to their convictions. I've learned to ignore them."

Linda, a 36-year-old biochemist, says her father, a widower, occasionally expresses concern about her being "an old maid." Pressure from her married friends comes in the form of frequently verbalized wishes that she would find "someone wonderful."

"Is it too late for me?" Linda asks. "Is this the price one pays for independence and a strong sense of self?"

A 31-year-old kindergarten teacher says that whenever she is seriously dating someone, her mother becomes emotionally committed to the relationship and tries to help her "get him." Both parents start asking when they can expect a wedding and grandchildren. "My responses vary depending to my mood," she reports. "I tell them not to worry about it, or I just don't answer. Often I ask, How come you don't nag my brother this way?"

She is not the only one who mentions different treatment accorded to male family members. "On holidays when our relatives get together, the pressure is always on all us single females to get ourselves husbands as fast as possible," reports a Midwest woman.

"But naturally, the single males are not urged to get wives."

And one woman, Ruth, carries a burden of guilt from what is perhaps the most extreme and saddest expression of maternal angst. On her deathbed, Ruth's mother turned to her and murmured, "If only you were married, so I could die in peace." Those were the last words Ruth ever heard her mother say.

Those are the voices of women who have no "significant other" in their lives. Is the pressure any less, or more, for a woman in a committed relationship?

Peggy is 29 and has had a steady boyfriend for six years. "My mother says she will pay for my wedding and keeps upping the ante. At weddings, people come up and say, 'Well, you're next.' Every holiday, my family asks if Mark and I are engaged, and a lot of my friends seem to feel it's helpful to point out that we've been dating a long time. I even get it from my doctor—as he puts it, my biological clock is ticking," Peggy says. "I try to shrug all this off, but frankly, I get knots in my stomach."

Susan is a legal secretary who plans to go on to law school. She has dated one man exclusively for two years. She reports pressure not from her mother but from everybody else—her stepfather, other relatives, single friends, married friends, and co-workers. They make seemingly innocent remarks such as, "I thought you two got married" or "Aren't you married yet?" Susan shrugs it off, denies any intention of getting married at this time. "It's my life, and I intend to make a very careful choice if I decide to marry," she says.

Another 29-year-old woman has lived with her lover for two years, but both her mother and her lover's family, who live in different cities, are unwilling to consider the relationship a solid one. "We always visit our parents together, but they act as if we are just dating, and won't let us sleep in the same room," she reports. How do she and her lover handle it? "We give in."

Some parents whose unmarried children live with their lovers are able to accept the situation when it's not under their noses, but still cannot deal with it in their own homes. No matter how commonplace, no matter how socially tolerated it is, their children's unwed sexuality makes them uncomfortable. Many young people, like the couple above, accommodate their parents' preference more or less gracefully.

Joan's situation is complicated and often stressful. At 31, Joan is an account executive at a West Coast advertising agency. She has lived with her lover for six years and would like to marry him. He however is unwilling—he likes the arrangement just as it is. Pressure on Joan from her parents, other relatives, and many of her friends is, not surprisingly, considerable.

"I have been urged to end the relationship and put myself on the market for a man who is willing to make a marital commitment," she concedes. "In the eyes of my religious parents, I've compromised my 'moral character' by living with my lover without marriage. And since I myself would prefer to be married, I feel I've compromised my feminist values by agreeing to this non-marriage marriage.

"When people make comments or suggestions about it, I either feel annoyed that they're poking their noses into my privacy, or terribly uneasy that they may be right. Depending on my mood or the state of my relationship at that moment, I simply wish they'd leave me alone, or I feel confused and uncertain as to whether I agree with them. This is something I've got to work out with my lover and within myself. Interference from others doesn't help me."

Mary, a 40-year-old television executive, has lived with her lover for nearly a year. He is unwilling at this point to get married. She is happy in the relationship, and while she would be willing to marry him, she is content not to push him. Her immediate family does not pressure her, but other relatives and friends make it their business to remind her that if she wants children, she had better marry soon. "I would like children, but I value my relationship with my lover more, and we are committed to each other. Advice and comments are not welcome," Mary says.

Several of the women who responded to the survey for this book seem to want to marry not so much for their own sakes, and not just to put an end to pressure from others, but to please people they care about. Dr. Janet Hall, a New York City psychiatrist whose patients include many single women, says this is not a rare situation—people do sometimes marry mainly to please others.

"It would be nice for my mother to see me share my life with someone," one woman states. "On some level, I feel obligated to be married, for others as well as for myself."

A 29-year-old puts it this way: "My family and my married friends take a keen interest in whatever efforts I make to meet men and in how I approach relationships with men as they develop. Their preoccupation with my social life often makes me feel I must be doing something wrong, and that I am disappointing them. This exacerbates the pressure I put on myself in trying to please them."

Nancy

At 32, Nancy is an assistant district attorney in an East Coast city. She lives alone, is currently dating several men. She expects to be practicing law even if she were to marry, though perhaps not at the same job.

She does not report pressure to marry from her family; her experiences are from the workplace. "I formerly worked in an office with mostly men and a few women, all 50 years old or over. Most of them couldn't understand why I wasn't married, or at least divorced. Several of the men told me I *needed* a husband, and that I'd better hurry up. One of the women even started telling lies about me, accusing me of being a lesbian. (I filed a grievance and won.)

"I really think the generation gap is severe when it comes to equality for women," Nancy continues. "Older people find it very difficult to accept independent behavior from a young woman.

"It can be very hard on one's confidence to be questioned about not being married—or not having ever been married. I think many people still measure a woman's success in terms of her marital status. In the past, having been divorced was a stigma; now I think the single/never married status is becoming as much stigmatized as being divorced used to be.

"Right now I have a boyfriend and I feel good about my attractiveness as a woman. But when I don't have a boyfriend, and people ask me why I'm not married, I feel a twinge of inadequacy, as if maybe I'm not desirable.

"I think it's important to have role models—women we can admire who never married. It's necessary for all of us to see that they are complete, fulfilled, and happy."

Hall agrees that women's perceptions of themselves once they have been married are different from those of women who have never been married, perhaps because of society's attitude that they have at least once followed tradition and have earned approval for it. "Many women feel an urgency to attain the status of marriage, and are more relaxed once they have had it, even if it didn't last," she says. "Never-married women may even envy divorced women for having at least experienced marriage, as if it were a goal that they themselves have not achieved."

Nancy's comment about women role models raises an interesting point about the way feature stories in the media depict prominent, high-achieving women. Magazine and newspaper articles are unusually quick to point out the women's married status, and their children, if any—as if to reassure readers that these are indeed "normal" women who, in spite of their success, have not rejected their "true" roles. Women's magazines will frequently have such a woman photographed not at her job but cozily at home surrounded by her children, even though the focus of the story is on her career achievements.

True, many writers of such articles may be making the point that accomplished women, if they have also managed a family, are doubly to be admired for having done two jobs successfully. But conversely, prominent women who are single are sometimes subliminally portrayed as somewhat lonely and unfulfilled.

When Molly Yard was elected president of the National Organization For Women in 1987, some newspapers reported the event thus: "Grandmother Elected President." As biologist Michael Zimmerman asked in an article in the *National N.O.W. Times,* why was Yard's reproductive status of such paramount importance? In the case of a male executive, would newspapers run a headline such as, "Grandfather Appointed Secretary of Defense," or "Grandfather to Head General Motors"?

Amy

Amy, 33 years old, is the director of women's athletics at a college. She confesses that she is not dating—"I'm extremely shy and self-conscious around men"—yet she has wide interests and the picture that emerges of her is of a competent woman leading an active and quite happy life. She has several pets and her own horse, goes to concerts, opera, and films, spends most of her free time

2

Mothers

"Twenty-two
was just
right"

It's not easy to be a mother—sometimes it seems as if whatever she does, it's wrong. Her worries, her concerns are suspect simply because she *is* a mother. Her advice is usually thwarted, especially because it is freely given. To her adult daughter, it is particularly difficult for a mother to refrain from offering advice if the daughter is, as she perceives it, misdirected and vulnerable—in other words, unmarried.

In terms of the subject of this book, it might be well to ask what it once meant to be a mother. The changes that have occurred within that role could account for many of the differences between mothers and daughters in their expectations and priorities concerning marriage.

The cult of motherhood that our society has inherited affirms the patriarchal ideal that every woman is biologically, instinctively prepared to be concerned first and foremost with loving a man and being loved by him, to admire and serve him. She presumably ensures being cherished by him by having his children. She becomes "fulfilled" by having children and devoting herself to her supreme biological purpose of child care.

But by achieving her role as mother, she becomes dependent, defeated as a self-sufficient person. In the past, when the availability and efficiency of birth-control methods were uncertain, a woman had to be assured of economic support at least throughout her childbearing years.

The consequences of these attitudes have been summarized by Dr. Conalee Levine-Schneidman and Karen Levine in their book, *Too Smart for Her Own Good?*:

"The fact that women relied on men for money meant that they relied on men for all of the things money symbolized: status, authority, and ultimately, even identity. And implicit in women's reliance on men for all of those things was their acceptance of a deferential position in their intimate relationships. Consciously or unconsciously, they knew on which side their bread was buttered. They may have acted as though they were independent, but the bottom line indicated otherwise. Women were locked into a system of economic dependency, and the truth is that they were only as independent as the confines of that system allowed."

Unconsciously and unintentionally, many of today's mothers gave their daughters these messages when they were growing up. Even if they did not explicitly say as much, their behavior and life situations made the lessons plain to their daughters. These mothers may have fostered ambition, independence, and assertiveness—"Get an education and be successful at a career." But when their daughters remained single, their panic undermined the conviction of their encouragement. "You should get married!" they now proclaimed, meaning, "Find a good provider, someone who will take care of you."

Thus, some mothers of unmarried women are so preoccupied with their daughters' singlehood that they become ambivalent about the very careers they once cheered onward. If a daughter telephones her mother in great excitement with news of a hard-earned promotion at work, an advancement that means more money, responsibility, and satisfaction, will her mother share her elation? Even if she does, her reaction may well be tempered with worry and doubt. She might say, "That's nice, dear," and launch into a description of the wedding of a friend's daughter. So despite her daughter's financial independence, despite the fact that she is accepted, tolerated, even admired for her energy and skill, there's a gnawing concern that her daughter's life might be "barren"—even an anxiety that her daughter might be considered, in a way, a failure.

As noted earlier, mothers rank numerically second to other relatives as the source of pressure that unmarried woman report. It is because of the position mothers hold in their daughters' galaxy of relationships that their views matter so much. The emotionally charged desire for parental approval seems abiding. By adopting a different lifestyle, implicitly a partial rejection of her mother's wisdom, a daughter feels she risks losing her mother's love as well.

Her mother, coming from a different cultural context, is unable to give the kind of support for her lifestyle the daughter seeks, and therein lies the kind of miscommunication that leads to an uncomfortable resolution.

The results of the survey might shed light on where these mothers are coming from.

Their Backgrounds

Over half of the mothers who responded to the survey for this book were married by the time they were 22 years old. Some had married in their teens, but most did so in their early 20's. Few had been over 30 when they married.

It would be tempting to conclude that mothers who married before they were 30 are likely to worry about daughters who are still single at that age. Surprisingly, perhaps with the knowledge of hindsight, the mothers surveyed did not necessarily regard 30 as a critical age for their daughters' prospects of marrying. Instead, a substantial number felt that they themselves were too young when they married. Others, while they still feel that their marriage at a young age was just right for *them*, are aware that times have changed, and they don't necessarily expect their daughters to follow their example. "Twenty-two was just right for the time—1946," said one mother. "Twenty was right for me—not for everyone," explained another.

While the ages of the mothers surveyed cover a considerable range, the results conform to patterns established in several other demographic studies that indicate that American couples were marrying younger 30 or 40 years ago. With the focus of marriage on the creation of a family, it was simply taken for granted that women would marry while still in their prime for motherhood. The survey partially confirms this pattern: Only a few mothers sampled had only one child; the majority had between two and five children. Approximately one-half have at least one married child, and about half have grandchildren.

Between the 1950s and 1970s, the average age at which women married for the first time rose by one and one-half years. This trend parallels the increased economic and job opportunities that opened up for women in the same period. (The number of first marriages tends to drop with increased job opportunities.)

Education also seems to have had an impact on whether or not to marry. In 1972, approximately one-fifth of women between 35 and 40 years of age who had college degrees or an income of $20,000 or more had not married, in high contrast to only 5 percent of women in the same age bracket without college educations. This suggests that the rise in marrying age has been influenced by the fact that many women want to finish their education before marrying. It does not, however, rule out another possibility—that many men may be unwilling to marry women of high education and earning power.

Today's educated women in their 30's have another phenomenon to contend with in terms of their marriage chances: the fact that traditionally, women have always tended to marry men at least a few years older than themselves—and to a large extent, they still do. Because the number of women has constantly risen in relation to the number of men, women born during the "baby boom" of the 1950s, during which this trend accelerated, have a proportionately smaller pool of possible mates to choose from among the men born just ahead of them.

The mothers who answered the questionnaires for this book, although aware that marrying ages have risen in the population generally, have not fully realized that daughters in their 30's are at a disadvantage numerically in terms of potential spouses. In 1987, there are many more women in their 30's than there are men of a few years older. This differential alone does not explain why fewer educated women are marrying today, or why the daughters who speak here are single, but it is a factor that mothers who are urging their daughters to marry seem not to take into consideration. Times have not only changed in terms of marrying age—their daughters are also caught in a marriage squeeze.

Not surprisingly, the survey revealed a connection between a mother's own marital happiness and the degree to which she worries about her unmarried daughter. Indeed, all of the mothers who frequently worry about their daughters' futures would marry the same men again. Of the mothers who never worry, only about half would marry the same men again, while a third would not.

This certainly suggests that a mother, having found the security of a marriage relationship and a sense of accomplishment in raising a family, wants the same for her daughter. But that is a judgment that may have to be qualified: Her idea of happiness is likely to be linked to the economic security that the marriage provided. She also may not be able to envision a woman being happy without a husband. The culture in which she was nurtured had a sharply focused image of what constituted a happy woman: one who was immersed in her husband's interests and family life. Her own individuality was secondary to and limited by the home she created. As one 28-year-old daughter complained on her questionnaire, her parents and other relatives *assumed* she was unhappy—or at least, not truly happy and fulfilled, a postulate she resented.

A survey taken in 1986 by *Woman's Day,* one of the largest-circulation women's magazines in the world, drew 60,000 responses; only half of those women agreed that they would marry the same men if they had it to do over; 38 percent wouldn't, and 12 percent were unsure. Yet, among the mothers surveyed for this book, two-thirds would stick with the husbands they have (or, if widowed, the same spouses they'd had). Very few mothers are divorced; the majority are either still married or are widowed.

The notion of happiness for a woman being inextricably linked to marriage was reinforced by the results of the question on the survey of whether a woman had to be married in order to be happy. Forty percent of the mothers who would marry their husbands again agreed with this hypothesis. Of the mothers who said they would not remarry their spouses, none believe a woman's happiness is predicated on marriage. As might be expected, they worry less about their daughters' unmarried state than happily married mothers do.

One divorced mother, a professional, said she never worries about her unmarried 29-year-old daughter. "She is in a relationship at present that seems satisfying to her. I don't think her marital status is an important factor in her life at this time," she wrote.

Another mother, Rhoda, a social worker in a southern city, is married but indicated that in the light of present circumstances, she would not choose the same spouse again—"He has become increasingly withdrawn and totally involved in his work," she wrote. "Also, I recently discovered ten years of infidelity, which shocked and depressed me."

Rhoda never worries about her unmarried daughter. "I personally don't think there's any prestige in being married, and I believe she feels the same way. She doesn't mix in the kind of social circles that rate being married as the ultimate success for a woman." She added that she would like to be closer to her daughter and discuss her relationships with her, but "I respect her privacy."

Education

Approximately half of the mothers surveyed have college degrees. Because higher education is thought to be generally linked to non-traditional views of marriage and sex roles, it might be expected that college-educated mothers would worry less about their unmarried daughters. But analysis of the surveys shows that while the college-educated mothers have less traditional views of marriage generally, they worry just as much about their unmarried daughters. They may have lower expectations of marriage in the abstract, but they still want husbands for their daughters.

Further, no matter what their own level of education, mothers are more likely to worry more about their daughters if the daughters have post-graduate degrees. The higher a daughter goes in her education level after college, the higher her mother's anxiety level. Women who have done post-graduate work have usually often put their careers ahead of their social lives, thereby generating uneasiness in their mothers. Also, it was not so long ago that a college education was viewed by many as "wasted" on a woman because it was not deemed necessary to her in her expected role as housewife and mother. Today, even if a mother takes it for granted that her daughter will earn a Bachelor's degree, she may perceive an advanced degree as a threat to her marriage chances. There still exists strong evidence that many men are intimidated and uncomfortable, perhaps not so much with intelligence itself but with women who have higher education and superior jobs to show for it.

Nevertheless, the mother of a woman with a Master's or Ph.D. seems to keep her increased anxiety to herself. Even if she believes her daughter's higher education has narrowed the field of acceptable spouses for her, she apparently doesn't put any more heat on her daughter than she did when her daughter had only her Bachelor's. Since the energy and effort involved in acquiring a post-graduate degree is considerable, the mother of a woman who has achieved one may well have mixed feelings of concern and pride—concern because her child has not conformed but has challenged woman's traditional sociological place, pride because of the achievement itself.

While highly educated mothers and less educated mothers worry about the same about their daughters' chances of marrying, the survey revealed that a mother's own education level does make a difference in how much her daughter feels pressured. Daughters of less educated women reported feeling much less pressure from their mothers than women whose mothers' education level was as high or higher than their own.

One reason for this might be that a mother who has only a high school education, or less, could feel somewhat inhibited by her college-educated daughter's achievements. She might figure her bright daughter must know what she's doing, and at least can support herself. Because of the gap in their shared experiences, the less educated mother could feel she's not capable of advising her daughter, so despite her private worry, she hesitates to exert pressure.

The better educated mother, however, may be more comfortable discussing her daughter's relationships. She is accustomed to voicing her opinions, and may articulate her concern to her daughter, causing the daughter to feel pressured.

So according to the survey results, a highly educated mother and a less educated mother both worry whether their daughter will marry, and both worry more if she has more than a college degree. But the highly educated woman's daughter is more likely to feel pressure from her mother.

Consider these examples:

Vivian

Vivian is a high school principal whose 30-year-old daughter is an architect. She sometimes worries about her daughter, hopes she will marry because she doesn't want her to be lonely, and thinks she will regret not marrying when she is older.

On the list of reasons daughters give for why their mothers pressure them to marry, however, Vivian's daughter checked "She thinks marriage is a better measure of success for a woman than a good career is"; "She wants to be able to tell her friends that her daughter is getting married"; "She doesn't want me to be lonely"; "She would like grandchildren"; and "She feels that by remaining single I am implicitly rejecting her own position as wife and mother." And furthermore, according to Vivian's daughter, "She thinks I should marry because it is the thing to do."

Margaret

Margaret is an obstetrician, mother of a 28-year-old sales manager who has lived with her lover for several years. Margaret confesses to worrying about her daughter's unmarried state, yet says she does not talk about it to her. Nevertheless, her daughter, while she realizes her mother only wants the best for her, feels pressured—"She often makes a lot of general comments about marriage, and about how much she would like grandchildren."

Sylvia

A secretary with just a high school education, Sylvia is very proud of her 35-year-old daughter Karen, who has a Master's degree in fine arts and is the director of an art museum.

Sylvia indicated that she frequently worries about her daughter because she believes Karen often puts her career above her personal life. Sylvia thinks Karen would be happier married, and will regret not marrying when she is older. She says Karen rarely discusses her relationships with her, but "when she has a serious relationship, I know we'll discuss it." Meanwhile, Sylvia says she does not express her concerns to her daughter, a statement that is confirmed by Karen. "My mother never pressures me about marrying and is always supportive of my goals and decisions," she reports.

"I'd like it if she were seeing someone special, but it's her business," says Sylvia.

Sylvia feels that jobs and careers were closed to her when she was young because of her sex. She envies the career options young women have today.

She is, however, a great believer in marriage. "At all stages in life, I feel we need someone special and committed to us to share our successes and failures," she says. Sylvia was widowed, is now remarried. She agrees that the expectations of young men and women today are different—"Relationships are much more equal partnerships than when I was first married."

This mother believes her daughter is perfectly comfortable being single. "Karen says at present she is too busy for a serious relationship—she is very career-oriented. If and when she feels something is missing in her life, she'll do something about it. I don't think she'll have any problems," Sylvia states.

She believes strongly that women should not have children outside of marriage. When asked how she would feel if her daughter did, she expressed concern about the financial and other difficulties of raising a child alone. However, she indicated that she would certainly be supportive.

Asked on the survey if she feels her daughter should be doing more to find a suitable partner, Sylvia replies, "I would certainly like her to have someone, but the most important thing is for her to feel happy within herself."

Mothers and Jobs

Very few of the mothers surveyed for this book had been full-time homemakers while their children were growing up—most were employed, at least part time. In this respect, they were different from the majority of their peers: Twenty years ago, only a third of American mothers were in the workforce. And especially in the middle class, most women of that time viewed the workplace as marginal or irrelevant to them, and jobs as supplementary or contingent, rather than as avenues of stimulation and self-expression. The married middle-class woman could usually choose not to work. Further, a decision to give up working would be greeted with far more social support than any arrangement she made to balance work with her life at home.

Perhaps because of the traditional image of the ideal female role, mothers who were full-time homemakers when their children were young are more likely to worry about their daughters' marriage chances than are mothers who worked outside the home. Because they themselves were financially dependent on husbands, they are not as confident about women's earning ability as are those mothers who are or were employed. Certainly today's society still does not provide many examples of women who have risen to the tops of their professions equally with men.

Yet, a few of the daughters who responded to the survey earn as much or more than their parents' total family income. Since this would eliminate one very understandable reason for a mother to worry about her daughter ("I worry about her providing for herself economically"), might not the mothers of high-income daughters be somewhat less concerned about their marrying?

The survey indicated the opposite. The mothers of women who have surpassed them economically are slightly *more* concerned about their marrying. Their mistrust of the workplace is ironically expressed in their misperceptions of their daughters' achievements: These mothers think their daughters are higher up in their careers than the daughters consider themselves to be.

The paradox of the increased anxiety in the mother of a high-income woman might be that she believes potential husbands will feel threatened by her daughter's success and earning power, and in this she may not be altogether wrong. While a man might feel there's a certain cachet to being the escort or date of a visibly successful woman, he might hesitate to enter a permanent partnership in which he could imagine himself playing second fiddle. Since income so often dictates where ultimate power lies, a man with a low or average salary would have to be very strong and very liberated to feel equal and comfortable in a marriage with a very high-earning woman. Some marriage counselors point out that men who grew up in traditional households too often equate their salaries with their masculinity.

"Men have been conditioned to desire women who appear powerless," wrote sociologist John Gagnon in *Working Mother* magazine. "A lover or wife who is a success can seem profoundly threatening. Women who . . . take on new roles in the outside world challenge men's erotic prerogatives."

If powerlessness seems sexy to men, then women who try to make their mark are likely to be accused of being masculine for developing and displaying traits that have been preempted by men: persistence and drive, dedication, aggressiveness, and emotional detachment.

Some of the mothers surveyed were, or are, professionals or working in an administrative or managerial capacity. Most, however, have or previously had jobs that rank lower on a career scale than their daughters occupy today. The work experience of these mothers has been quite different from that of their daughters—less rewarding, less interesting, lower paid.

And so it is not surprising that the mothers differed greatly from their daughters in their attitudes toward their work. They showed less career commitment. Almost all the daughters expect to be working continuously for the next 15 years, regardless of the possibility that they might marry and have children. Many look forward to advancing in their fields. Like most educated women today, they think in terms of careers.

On the other hand, their mothers' approach to work was likely to be as a temporary situation until marriage or as a job to earn extra money, ancillary to their major role as wife and full-time mother. One mother who had not worked outside the home was amused at the question on the survey: "Until you retired, what was your occupation?" "Housewife—we never retire," she quipped.

Though some mothers who held relatively low-ranking jobs while their children were young went on to higher positions later, most were not interested in careers. This accounts for the difficulty that some mothers of ambitious, high-achieving women have in understanding their daughters' dedication to their work. One university study comparing the lifestyle commitment of women in 1970 and in 1980 categorized the various lifestyles as "family-directed, family-accommodated, career-accommodated, and career-directed." While in 1970 more than three-fourths of the women sampled chose family-directed, family-accommodated lifestyles, by 1980 only half of them did, and twice as many chose career-directed lifestyles as those who did in 1970.

Other studies have shown that great changes in women's attitudes toward their work, financial responsibility, and the division of labor within the home took place in the early 1970s. Mothers are certainly aware objectively that most women are now employed out of the home, and that many have advanced in careers once totally dominated by men. However, they seem not to have internalized these changes in terms of being able to fully understand their own daughters' investment in their careers. A number of mothers surveyed for this book expressed some concern about their daughters working too hard or sacrificing personal life for their jobs, without acknowledging that this is usually the way career goals are achieved—something their daughters care about greatly.

Asked if they worked while the children were young because they wanted to, or because the family needed the money, or if they would have preferred to stay home, many of the mothers would have stayed home, especially those who had jobs characterized as being faceless, without any chance for personal expression or creativity. A few chose to work even though their families didn't need the income; some mothers said both—they preferred to work *and* their families needed the money.

Mothers certainly recognize that their daughters have greater career opportunities than they themselves had. Or, as one mother put it, "I'm not sure I had fewer opportunities, but I certainly had less incentive."

One question on the mothers' survey asked, "How would you categorize the options you faced for your future when you were young?" The first answer that could be checked was, "I had many options, including marriage and a family, which did not limit my other options in any way." A Boston mother commented with irony, "Show me one women who checks this!"

Does this mean they envy their daughters because more doors are open to them? "Of course!" another mother answered.

"I wanted to go to medical school," said Doris, a pediatric nurse. "It was impossible because I had no encouragement or support from either my parents or my husband."

Envy, of course, does not necessarily mean begrudge. It's entirely possible that a mother might wish she had had the career options her daughter has—and at the same time, be sincerely happy that her daughter has them. But according to the survey for this book, that same mother is also likely to worry about her daughter's chances of marrying. In fact, the analysis of the surveys showed that mothers who worry the most do envy the opportunities open to their daughters.

Mothers who agree that they missed out on career opportunities may at the same time believe that such options would have interfered with personal or family situations. They may recognize that they could not have pursued the careers they wanted without considerably threatening other factors in their lives, as Doris indicated. Thus, they may translate their experience into assuming that their daughters' expanded options in careers will interfere with their ability to develop relationships that lead to marriage.

Vera, a Cleveland mother who has never worked outside the home since she married, greatly regrets the career opportunities that were closed to her when she was young because of her sex and also from lack of support from her family for her goals. Marriage and children seemed her only real options. She married at 22 and feels it was too young, is not sure she would marry the same man if she had it to do over again. Yet, despite these misgivings, Vera worries considerably about her unmarried 30-year-old daughter.

It's also possible, even probable, that many men of the mothers' generation would have been much more opposed to women creating or seizing career opportunities than men are today. Remembering this, mothers may not recognize that while many, maybe most, men today are apparently still uncomfortable with high-achieving women, others in fact are accustomed to them—and some even admire them without feeling threatened. When one 50-year-old New York woman, an executive in a large publishing company, announced to her family that her husband had just been made a vice-president of his firm, he put his arm around her and proudly reminded her family that after all, *she* had been a vice-president for years.

Helen

Married 40 years and the mother of three, Helen is a retired librarian living in Massachusetts. She worked part time when her children were young. She feels that there were social conditions in her day that made it hard for women to achieve and so chose a career in a field in which there was less discrimination—"It didn't occur to me that there was a choice," she says.

Helen believes there is a shortage of men and that young professional women today have too high standards for prospective husbands, that their high status is intimidating to men, that they enjoy their independence, and that men today expect women to give up too much for marriage.

Nevertheless, she is confident that her 37-year-old unmarried daughter would be married if she wanted to be. "She has had plenty of suitors and proposals. Obviously marriage is not her highest priority or she would be married," says Helen.

While Helen believes that marriage today is less important for a woman than it used to be, she worries sometimes—she thinks her daughter would be happier married and she doesn't want her to be lonely. However, she says she does not often express her concern. Her daughter reports that she knows her mother wants her to be happy and settled, but she does not feel pressured.

Helen says that her daughter occasionally talks to her about her dates and romantic involvements. Asked if she would like to discuss them more, Helen replies, "Perhaps, if it would contribute to her happiness. She has a right to decide for herself what is right for her, and discussion may or may not help."

Congratulations

Evidence of the disparity between mothers' and daughters' regard for careers was reinforced by answers to the question on the daughters' survey: "If you were very excited because you had just received especially high compliments on a project at work or were told about a promotion, who would be the first person you would want to call with the news?"

The most common response the daughters gave was "best friend," followed by "lover." This is hardly surprising; surely a contemporary, someone of one's own generation, is more likely to fully understand today's work scene. Also, a woman's best friend or lover (in some cases, one and the same person) would in all probability be up-to-date on the daily events of her career, might even work in the same field. The friend or lover would be aware of the effort that went into the job, and the full meaning of the recognition she received.

A mother is at a disadvantage here in that she most likely did not work at the same kind of job as her daughter, or even in the same field, and does not totally get the picture. Also, she may not have worked for many years, and therefore she can't really appreciate the competitiveness and harshness of many career fields today.

Nevertheless, some mothers seem to be insensitive. Daughters were asked, "If you called your mother with this news (of the praise or promotion), can you describe what her reaction would probably be?"

A number of answers were flatly negative: "Somewhat forced enthusiasm"; "Positive but with a lack of enthusiasm and sincerity"; "Emoting a lot in a not-so-genuine way"; "Superficial pleasure with an underlying sense of being threatened."

An Atlanta daughter reports, "She would congratulate me and tell me she's proud of me, and that would be it—we'd probably never discuss the subject again. She's not truly interested, she just goes through the motions."

According to one daughter, her mother would only be able to relate to the news in a totally pragmatic fashion: "Oh, that's nice. Is it more money?" thus discouraging any discussion of what the compensation might mean in other than monetary ways.

Another daughter, who is a nursery school teacher, wears her most casual clothes on her job. She says that if she reported a promotion or other recognition, her mother's first question would be whether she could now wear nice clothes to work. "And then she'd want to know what my boyfriend said."

Joan, the advertising agency executive, says her mother would be ecstatic but would add, "I just *knew* this would happen—I've been praying for you!" Prayer may be all to the good, but in this context it implies that it was divine interference, rather than the daughter's own competence and effort, that brought about the reward.

And a New York woman predicts her mother's reaction this way: "She'd say, 'Oh, that's great, babe!' And then, because she doesn't really understand what I do, she'd ask, 'What is the job, again?' And finally, she'd want to be reassured that I'm not leaving the city—'You're not moving, are you?' "

The reactions some daughters expect to receive indicate that their mothers lack confidence in their abilities: "She would wonder if I could handle the job. She'd ask, 'Why take on so much?' "

Lynn jokes a little about her mother's probable reaction: "She would be very pleased and proud, but she'd also tell me to work harder so 'they' wouldn't think they'd made a mistake. Mom operates on the theory that I'm pulling off a fast one and am going to be discovered."

However, some of the anticipated responses could reflect not so much a lack of confidence in the daughters' abilities as expressions of the mothers' worry. "If my daughter becomes more involved in her work," a mother might reason, "she will be even more inclined to put it ahead of personal life, and be less interested in seeking a romantic involvement that could lead to marriage."

"My mother would be excited and proud, but she would also express some cautious optimism, wanting to be sure there was no downside risk to my personal life," says Laura, an anesthesiologist.

Nevertheless, most of the daughters' speculations about their mothers' reactions to hearing good news about their careers was warmly positive. There was plenty of evidence that daughters could expect support and pride.

"'Good work, honey—I'm proud of you!'—that's what my mother would say," reports a Denver woman.

"She'd share my happiness and be supportive and proud," states Nancy.

"My mother would be thrilled, asking for details, telling my Dad about it while we were on the phone," reports a Portland woman. "She'd even plan a family dinner to celebrate."

"She'd be happy for me, and want to know the details, not just that it had happened," says another.

Kate, a medical librarian, also feels she could count on the right reaction. "My mother would be pleased and say it is no less than I deserve. She'd want to know the details and ramifications."

And perhaps one of the nicest comments from a daughter went like this: "My mother would be proud and happy for me. Since she hasn't worked in years, she might not understand the complete significance, but she would think it was terrific."

Evelyn

Evelyn is a bank manager, divorced, mother of four children, grandmother of one. She worked when her children were young because the family needed the extra income, but she would have preferred to stay home.

She makes the distinction between "envying" and "wishing"—"I do not envy the career and educational opportunities open to young women today," Evelyn says, "but I wish they had been available to me."

Her 35-year-old unmarried daughter has had a steady boyfriend for several years but does not expect to marry him. "She has confided his attitude about marriage and his reasons to me," says Evelyn. "I like him. But the important thing is her own feelings."

She admits that she worries sometimes that her daughter might be lonely some day, and thinks she would like to have children, but does not express her concern to her daughter, or try to introduce her to other people or pressure her. (Her daughter confirms everything this mother says, including that she discusses most aspects of her relationship with her mother.)

Evelyn does not think her daughter is too picky—"She must make her own choice as to the suitability of a partner."

3

Communications

"She

doesn't

understand"

"I don't have an open and direct relationship with my mother," says a daughter.

"I would like to hear more about my daughter's life, but she becomes defensive if I question her," says a mother.

Such refrains were not uncommon in the surveys returned by mothers and daughters for this book. Although many mother/daughter pairs felt they had a warm and close relationship, still others indicated there was a communication gap between them.

*"Mis*communication" may be responsible for the strained relations between some of these women. Many of the paired responses reveal a deep chasm of social change and cultural differences between mothers and daughters and their expectations about marriage as a means to happiness. A mother's most innocent query or casual remark may be interpreted by her daughter as carrying hidden messages about what she should or should not do. Even a mother's silence through some strange alchemy can be construed as pressure because a daughter infers too much from her mother's stoic concern. In some instances, a daughter may indeed hear a mixed message or cultural attitude that reflects her mother's upbringing and experience, which she'll then misinterpret as almost a selfish motive on the part of her mother. And, sometimes, the messages simply are not there.

The responses to the surveys revealed many discrepancies between what mothers think and what their daughters think they think. Nowhere was this gap more evident than in the reasons mothers gave for why their daughters should marry and the daughters' version of how it was coming across.

Why Mothers Worry

One of the questions the daughters' survey posed was what, in their opinion, were the main reasons that their mothers sometimes pressured them to marry. The answers were multiple choice: "She thinks you would be happier married"; "She thinks your life would be more stable"; "She thinks marriage is a better measure of success for a woman than a good career is"; "She doesn't want you to be lonely"; and several other possibilities (see **Appendices A and B**).

By and large, most daughters agreed that their mothers were thinking of their happiness and didn't want them to be lonely. Indeed, when mothers were offered almost identical choices of answers in their version of the survey, nearly all checked, "I don't want her to be lonely," as a principal reason for their worry.

But on other points, there were distinct differences between the mothers' reasons for wanting their daughters to marry and the daughters' perceptions of their mothers' reasons. For example, 44 percent of the daughters think their mothers want them to marry because of their desire for grandchildren. Yet only 12 percent of the mothers checked this as their reason for concern. One daughter checked only "(My mother) would like grandchildren" and "She wants to be able to tell her friends that her daughter is getting married." By excluding any other possible reasons, this seemed a bitter assessment of her mother's attitude and implies some kind of selfishness as part of her mother's motive. Could it be the daughters themselves want children but are projecting the feeling onto their mothers, disguising their own pronatal wish as a desire on their mothers' part for grandchildren?

However, though a relatively small number of mothers indicated wanting grandchildren as a reason they hoped their daughters would marry, the survey results indicated that women who have no grandchildren are more likely to worry about their unmarried daughters, and more likely to express their concern to them. And daughters of women with no grandchildren feel substantially more maternal pressure to marry.

As for marriage announcements, almost one-quarter of the daughters believe their mothers want to be able to tell friends that their daughter is getting married. Yet, not one mother checked this response. One mother explained that she was reluctant to answer this question for fear of being misunderstood: "I would be delighted to be able to tell my friends that my daughter is getting married, but I would feel selfish if I checked this. I want marriage for her only if she finds the man she really wants."

Some daughters are reading ulterior motives into their mothers' concern even when they don't exist. An example of such a misunderstanding turned up in one mother's reply: "I would like for *her* to have children." This woman had not checked "I would like grandchildren" on the list of reasons—she wished her daughter to experience the fulfillment she herself had felt in having children. Unless a mother who feels that way makes herself clear, a daughter could wrongly conclude that her mother's genuine wish for her daughter's pleasure and happiness is simply a desire for grandchildren.

A Denver mother made this interesting philosophical comment for hoping her daughter will marry and have children: "Competent people should have children to help maintain the next generation."

In many instances where variances showed up between the daughters' estimation of why their mothers sometimes pressure them to marry and their mothers' own statements of their reasons, it seems, as noted, that many mothers don't confess their worries to their daughters. And sometimes the daughters apparently discourage discussion on the subject. One mother who admitted she sometimes worries said she rarely tries to talk with her daughter about marriage. How does the daughter react when she does? "She cries," said the mother.

A comparison of the surveys also revealed that daughters may conceal their true feelings from their mothers. A Philadelphia mother reported that she frequently worries about her daughter's lack of a husband, and often expresses her concern to her daughter, though gently—she was quite emphatic that she never pushes, only suggests. She was insistent that she and her daughter are able to discuss the matter objectively, that they communicate very well. Nevertheless, the daughter reported that while she believes her mother only wants her to be happy, she becomes inwardly very anxious and angry when her mother brings up the subject of marriage.

A highly worried mother of a 34-year-old checked nearly all the reasons on the list in the survey: "I think she would be happier married"; "Her life would be more socially acceptable"; "I don't want her to be lonely"; "I think she will regret not marrying when she is older"; "I worry about her providing for herself economically"; "I would like grandchildren"; and added "I think some of her friends don't include her in social activities because she is single." This mother said she rarely expresses her concerns to her daughter because the daughter becomes defensive. However, the daughter indicated on her survey that she is acutely aware of her mother's anxiety and resents even the unspoken pressure.

Several mothers expressed ambivalence; they might think their daughters would be better off married, but at the same time they can relate to the way their daughters conduct their lives. A mother who said she frequently worries about her daughter checked, on the list of reasons: "I think she would be happier married"; "I think her life would be more socially acceptable"; "I don't want her to be lonely"; "I would like grandchildren"—and said she expresses her concerns to her daughter. "I think she really wants to be married," said this mother—and then added almost as an afterthought, "but she has spent many of her best years doing all the things that most of us would have liked to do, but didn't have the courage!"

As Professor Moira Crone wrote in an article in *Working Mother* magazine, "The popular culture of the early '50s did not encourage women to fulfill any of their needs or desires directly but through other people." Again, the mixed message: "Do as I always wanted to do but didn't, but on the other hand, do as I have done."

To the question of whether it makes them uncomfortable to tell people that their daughters are unmarried, the mothers overwhelmingly answered no. "It never makes me uncomfortable," said one mother, "although this has not always been true. Time changes attitudes. Today, marriage is regarded as less essential than it once was for a woman."

Younger/Older Daughters

It is not surprising that among the women surveyed for this book, fewer mothers of younger daughters worry than mothers of women in their late 30's and over 40. Those mothers of daughters under 30 who do worry say they only worry sometimes. Probably mothers of women under 30 assume that their daughters still have plenty of time to choose a husband.

Yet, pressure on a woman to marry may start even earlier. Dr. Hall recalls a 24-year-old who had just completed her Ph.D. and whose family immediately expected her to select a *high-functioning* man and marry him. The young woman came to Hall because she was having trouble coping with the pressure. "I can't treat you," Hall told her after examining her, "because you have no psychiatric problem—your reactions are entirely normal."

Birth order seems to have some effect on a mother's concern. The survey results indicated a slightly greater tendency for mothers to worry more about second daughters, and to put more pressure on them. If the older sibling is married, that leaves the younger as the only one left to worry about. On the other hand, if the older daughter is unmarried, the mother may regard the younger as a better bet for presenting her with grandchildren. Also, a mother may have higher expectations, in terms of accomplishment, of her firstborn, and if that daughter is indeed a high achiever, this may cause the mother to expect the younger sibling to follow more traditional patterns.

The survey does not indicate conclusively whether a mother's anxiety increases in direct proportion to her daughter's age. It would seem logical if this were so. Yet, mothers of older women might accept the fact that their daughters will probably remain single and learn to live with it comfortably. Therefore, it's possible that mothers of women in the middle age group—say, 31 to 34—worry the most.

What is interesting is that there is no dramatic difference among the daughters in the three age groups in terms of whether or not they *feel* pressured by their mothers. If the mothers of under-30 women are less worried about their daughters marrying, wouldn't it be safe to assume that these daughters feel less pressure? Not so, to hear the daughters tell it.

Dividing the women who responded into three groups—under 30, 31 to 34, and 35 and older—there was no major difference among them in whether they felt pressure from their mothers. About half the women in each age group said they do. So the natural question would seem: Why would a 27-year-old think her mother is pressuring her—especially if her mother is not particularly worried?

There are several possible answers. If the mother of a younger woman is actually beginning to worry, she might not verbalize her uneasiness to her daughter because it would seem premature. Yet, because she is concerned, this mother might reveal it not verbally but in the way she acts. Even what she *doesn't* say could tell her daughter a lot.

On the other hand, the young woman herself could be beginning to worry. She has heard about the man shortage, she is aware that the reservoir of suitable men shrinks as she gets older, but she has not accepted the possibility that she may never marry. She may imagine that her mother is pressuring her when actually the concern she feels is self-generated. And we've already seen that the question of having children as a prerequisite of womanhood is a very touchy issue for younger women trying to assess their options.

Another possibility is that younger women are unaccustomed to being pressured to marry, and therefore notice it and react to it. Older women may have experienced years of such pressure and know how to avoid it or are so used to it that they hardly notice it any more.

According to the survey, the majority of the women in the oldest age group are not currently dating. If mothers tend to think of dating as leading to marriage, it might be expected that the mothers of these women would worry more than mothers of younger women who are actively dating. However, of mothers who worry, about half of them have daughters who are seeing someone, and half have daughters who aren't.

At any rate, an older unmarried daughter may not feel any more, or less, pressured than a younger woman. In fact, the opposite often seems to be true. One 41-year-old executive says, "I don't get as much pressure from my mother, relatives, and co-workers now as I did when I was younger. The only real pressure I experience at this point in my life is when I notice that so many invitations among friends and acquaintances seem to be for couples. Then I feel left out." And she adds, "I've had to grow a thick skin, learn to use humor as a defense against showing my hurt."

A New York CEO, now in her early 50's, recalls that her mother abruptly stopped pressuring her when, at age 40, she had a mastectomy. "I guess she thought I was so damaged, nobody would ever want me," she says. "She was floored when I met and married Steve, five years ago. She said, 'Now I can die in peace!' I was taken aback and asked her what she meant. She said she'd been worried about my supporting myself! Here I was, a vice president, head of the biggest department of a huge corporate empire, and my mother thought I couldn't take care of myself. Of course, she'd never got the picture all along. As I was promoted in my career, she never paid enough attention to understand."

Apparently Ruth's mother is not the only one who speaks in terms of feeling able to die in peace only if a daughter is married.

Laura

This 35-year-old anesthesiologist has a younger sister and brother, both married. While her mother confesses to having some concern about her daughter, she does not express it to her, and Laura reports that she doesn't feel pressure to marry from her mother or anyone else. "I am viewed as the achiever in my family," she says.

She indicates that her mother is herself a fairly independent, efficient, and achievement-oriented person, and has always been supportive of her daughter's career plans and goals.

Her mother believes Laura is often depressed about not being married, but the daughter's survey does not bear this out. Laura is dating two people, but while she thinks she would like to date only one person at some point, she doesn't feel like making an exclusive commitment right now.

She would like to be dating more, but does occasionally put her career aspirations ahead of romantic involvements. Her five closest friends are women, both married and single.

She rarely talks to her mother about her romantic involvements. "I think she might like to hear more," Laura says, "but I am a reticent person and don't talk easily about personal feelings."

If she does not marry, Laura expects she will receive the emotional support and fulfillment she would need for a happy life from her close friends—"and from my children," she says, for even if she does not marry, she plans to adopt children. She says that lacking a supportive husband, she would employ household help to assist her in caring for the children.

Cathleen

Cathleen, a dental technician, has been married for over 40 years to a man she would still marry if she had the choice to make again. She has two married daughters, a married son, and three grandchildren. Her 29-year-old daughter Terry, a graphics designer, is her only unmarried child.

A woman who holds quite traditional views of marriage, Cathleen feels that marriage and a family were her only real options when she was young, yet she does not envy the career opportunities young women have today.

She believes that fewer young professional women are marrying these days because their standards and expectations of prospective husbands are too high and because their success is intimidating to men. She also observes that they make so much money they don't need to marry for financial security. (Terry sees it differently: She thinks professional women's careers don't allow time for much personal life, and that men are too demanding in what they expect women to give up for marriage.)

The gap between Cathleen's perception of her relationship with her daughter and her daughter's version of it is striking. Cathleen worries sometimes about the fact that Terry is unmarried but says she rarely expresses her concern. Terry says her mother, along with other relatives and married friends, pressures her about marriage. Cathleen's reasons for worrying are that she feels her daughter would be happier married, and if she doesn't marry will regret it when she is older. Terry agrees her mother worries about her for those reasons, but she also thinks her mother wants grandchildren, wants to be able to tell her friends that her daughter is getting married, and is concerned about her providing for herself economically.

Cathleen says that she and her daughter rarely discuss Terry's relationships, and that she never gives advice. Terry, however, states that she discusses most aspects of her relationships with her mother, and receives advice from her on just about everything except her career!

Talking About Relationships

Many relationships between mother and daughter were revealed in the survey as strained or remote especially when it comes to discussing the daughter's love life.

A question was asked: "Which of the following statements comes closest to describing the way you discuss your romantic involvements with your mother?" The choices offered were: "I usually discuss most aspects of my relationships with my mother"; "I talk about my relationships with my mother but I leave out any negative information such as bad habits of my partner or problems we are having"; and "I rarely talk to my mother about my relationships except to mention them in passing."

While some daughters reported that they often freely discuss their romantic relationships with their mothers, most said that they rarely do—or that they give a "sanitized" version. Mothers, asked if they wished to hear more than their daughters told them, gave mixed answers. Over half said they were content with whatever intimate discussions they have with their daughters, or that they would want to hear more only if their daughters indicated a wish to confide. Their comments attest that they do not pry:

"I would not like to discuss her relationships more than we do. It's her business unless she wishes to share something with me."

"I take my cue from her, to discuss or not discuss."

"Only if she initiates the discussion. She knows the lines of communication are open and it is easy to talk, but I usually let her begin, as I feel it is more comfortable for her that way."

"I would like to be closer to my daughter and discuss her relationships with her, but I respect her privacy."

In comparing questionnaires returned by mother/daughter pairs, it's evident that sometimes when a daughter gives her mother only a positive, partial version of her relationships, the mother understandably gets a distorted picture of the daughter's life. One mother confidently reported that she frequently talks to her daughter about her relationship with the man her daughter is dating exclusively; the daughter admitted giving only the good news.

On the other hand, another mother said she rarely talks to her daughter about her relationships—but according to the daughter, she tells her mother just about everything!

Some mothers, however, feel shut out. Interestingly, the analysis of the mothers' surveys suggests that mothers who worry most about their daughters' unmarried state are those whose daughters decline to talk to them about their relationships with their lovers or dates. "When I try to talk to my daughter about her relationships, she becomes emotional and thinks I am criticizing," reported one mother who worries frequently.

As for the daughters' reasons for withholding confidences, some claimed negative experiences when they had shared information with their mothers in the past. Here is what several of those daughters have to say about why they don't communicate:

"I don't trust her. She is too critical."

"When I reveal too much, my mother tends to use it against me when she gets angry."

Another daughter says that her mother would be shocked to learn she has a sex life. "And she'd probably disapprove of men I date. I don't want her judgments of my friends."

A few women mentioned knowing that their mothers did not approve of the sexual freedom enjoyed by women today. "Until I was in a committed relationship, I rarely talked to my mother about men I was seeing because I felt she didn't want to hear. Not being monogamous was liberating to me and helped me to grow, but my life probably just seemed promiscuous to her," one woman explains.

Even being in a monogamous relationship doesn't always help. One woman who lives with her lover adds, "I can't talk to my mother about my relationship with my boyfriend because she believes that it's wrong for a man and woman to live together without marriage."

"In the past, my mother has used incriminating evidence against me, when what I needed then was just moral support," reports another.

Lynn, the public relations executive who feels pressured by her pseudo-feminist sister, has the same problem. "When I talk to my mother about my relationships, I leave out any negative information. She has a marvelous ability to hit me with it years later. I once discovered that she could still recite, chapter and verse, everything that was wrong with a man I had been seriously involved with ten years earlier. That was when I learned to edit what I tell her," says Lynn.

Other daughters want to avoid criticism:

"My mother is very judgmental and would make known her disapproval. Our values in regard to relationships are very different."

"I feel we operate by rules so different that any meaningful discussion is unlikely."

"I don't trust her to understand and support me. I don't want her reactions."

Or, they put it more diffidently:

"I feel my mother would like to hear more, but I am uncertain of her reactions. I have a fear of intimacy with my mother."

"She is talkative, and I am very private about my personal life. I would not want her to discuss my private matters with her friends or business associates."

"She tends to assume more of a future in a relationship than is actually there and to ask questions I prefer not to answer."

And still other women don't communicate fully with their mothers because they want to protect them against unpleasantness. On both surveys, daughters and mothers were asked whether or not the daughter was currently seeing someone. Roughly a quarter of the mothers' answers were out of sync with their daughters'—they either said their daughters were not seeing someone when in fact the daughters indicated that they were, or vice versa.

Possibly, some daughters are afraid that if they tell their mothers that they are currently seeing someone special, their mothers will get their hopes up prematurely and, if the relationship breaks off, will be disappointed. Other daughters, for various reasons, may find it easier to let their mothers believe they are seeing someone, when actually they are not. (One mother who said her daughter was seeing someone was asked how she felt about him. "We like Michael very much," she wrote. Michael? Her daughter made no mention of Michael or anybody else, and in fact said she wasn't seeing anyone and wished she were dating.)

"Basically, my mother can't handle my problems. She worries too much," one daughter puts it.

"At one point I was ashamed of a relationship I had with a married man; another time, I was involved with a man whose background my mother would have disapproved of," says another woman. "Now, I have a lover with whom I have ups and downs. There is just no point in worrying her when I have a fight with him, or when I'm feeling uncertain about the relationship."

An Atlanta woman says she rarely talks to her mother about her relationships, even though she thinks her mother would like to hear about them. "She gets upset whenever I'm hurt or upset, so I avoid any such possibility by telling her very little about my dating. In the past, when I was badly hurt in a few relationships, she was supportive, but I felt that my own pain was awfully hard on her. Now, if I were dating someone I was in love with and could be confident the relationship would continue, I would discuss it with her." (Apparently while it's important for a mother to care, in these situations, it's unnerving if she cares too much.)

On the survey, daughters were asked how often they saw their mothers or spoke to them on the telephone. Whether they live in the same area or are separated by geography, most tended to stay in fairly close touch. Later, in telephone interviews with respondents, mothers and daughters were both asked about these calls: Who telephones whom? If it had turned out that the mothers were most often the ones who initiated the calls, this might be viewed as an additional expression of the mothers' anxiety, possibly one that daughters interpreted as pressure.

However, apparently this is not the case: The score is about even. Most mothers and daughters indicated that they more or less take turns. A few daughters said their mothers usually call them, but a few reported the opposite—they are more likely to call their mothers.

"We kick ideas around," reported one mother, "and I cheer her on."

Deborah

Deborah seems to have many of the problems of today's unmarried women. She not only feels pressure from several sources but alienation and lack of communication with her mother.

At 35, Deborah is a newspaper reporter, happy in her job, lives alone with her two cats, and is enrolled in a postgraduate course at a university. She sometimes puts her career aspirations ahead of her romantic interests. She was once engaged, but she and her partner both realized the relationship was a mistake. She is not currently dating anyone—"I'm interested in forming a long-term relationship but not in a series of unpredictable affairs."

Deborah thinks her mother would like to hear more about her life, but, "We don't have an open and direct relationship. She has never been any help in advising me or giving me an example of a satisfying relationship. I don't want the kind of relationship for myself that she has with my father—but I rarely get a chance to talk with her away from my father."

In Deborah's opinion, her mother pressures her to marry because she wants grandchildren and wants to tell her friends that her daughter is getting married. Further, Deborah has the impression that her mother thinks she is implicitly rejecting her own position as wife and mother by remaining unmarried.

"I think society generally expects a woman to marry, and judges her accordingly," Deborah sums up. "New acquaintances always want to know right off the bat if I'm married. I feel left out of conversations about husbands and children. And my mother occasionally makes remarks about how much she likes to play with the babies of my cousins. The message I get is that I have failed, and that she thinks she too has somehow failed."

How does this make her feel? "I feel like a failure. I feel people might think I'm gay. I feel old and ugly."

Perceptions

One part of the mothers' survey for this book dealt with their perceptions of how their daughters themselves feel about being unmarried. Whether or not the women verbalize their feelings to their mothers, the mothers were mixed in response to the question: "How do you think your daughter views being unmarried?"

"Regretfully," says a Denver mother succinctly.

"Comfortably," replies the mother of a 28-year-old.

"I believe she is very often lonely," replies an Oregon mother.

"She doesn't like it," a Philadelphia mother believes.

"She is happy single," says the mother of a 30-year-old.

"Though she never expresses it and is a 'correct-thinking' feminist, I believe she would like the security and companionship of being attached to one person," observes a New York mother.

The mother of a successful 35-year-old businesswoman comments, "I think she puts her self-fulfillment in a career with creative possibilities above the fulfillment that comes from marriage."

A comparison of mother/daughter surveys indicates that many mothers are correct in their assessment of their daughters feelings.

"I don't think she worries about being unmarried or gives much thought to it," said the mother of a 38-year-old executive. "I don't believe she is anti-marriage; if the right person came along and pursued her, I think she'd be interested. But she is well educated, independent, economically secure, and has a wide circle of friends, both married and single, and many interests. Her lifestyle seems to suit her very well. She does not express a need for marriage." According to the daughter's survey, this mother is pretty much on target.

"She is strong-willed and independent, and I understand that," another mother wrote. "I think she is content being single at this point in her life." Her daughter indicated she would perhaps like to be dating more than she is, but as for marrying, "I've been hurt in the past and rather than take a chance, I prefer to be alone at this time."

Other mothers believe their daughters wish very much to be married. It is hard to tell if they are reading their daughters correctly or are unconsciously projecting their own feelings, perhaps picturing their daughters' singlehood as lonely because they themselves would feel vulnerable and forlorn if they were unmarried.

Some surveys reveal that daughters may put up very good fronts before their mothers. One Michigan mother believed her daughter was very relaxed about being single. "It doesn't seem to bother her. I think she thoroughly enjoys being independent, living alone, and having a satisfying career," she said. However, her daughter's survey revealed a good deal of anxiety about her life and resentment at pressure she feels from her family and associates.

One mother of a 30-year-old woman says she never worries about her daughter marrying and never pressures her. Her daughter leads a busy, interesting life and is perfectly happy, according to this mother. She believes that she and her daughter communicate very well. The daughter, however, while confirming that her mother does not pressure her, nevertheless very poignantly expresses a longing to be married and have children. There seems to be a communication lapse in this mother-daughter relationship.

However, some mothers have picked up on two factors that partially answer the complex question: "Why isn't my daughter married?" These mothers recognize their daughters' selectivity in their choices, and they understand the cautiousness with which many unmarried women today view the institution of marriage. Their answers therefore are more qualified:

"I think my daughter is a very sincere person and feels that marriage is a strong commitment," says a St. Louis mother. "I believe she is afraid of the games married people play. Therefore, if she couldn't have a husband that she felt she could trust completely, she would rather be unmarried."

"She would rather be single than have an unhappy marriage," another mother reports.

"There are a lot worse things than being alone," observes a mother who is a professor at a Midwestern university. "I think my daughter is fairly comfortable with her life right now. But I do imagine she would enjoy being in a supportive, loving relationship—she has a lot to give."

Mothers in the survey who were divorced believe their unhappy experiences affect their daughters. Dr. Hall has seen in her practice that continual bickering on the part of parents sometimes turns children off marriage.

"She did not see a ,happy mother when she was growing up," a mother writes from California. "I think she'd like a close relationship but doubts that it can be achieved in marriage."

"I think my daughter views marriage as wonderful if with the right person," says a divorced southern mother. "But I think marriage scares her because she saw how tough it was on me and the rest of the children when my marriage to her father did not work out."

"I believe my daughter would love a child of her own. Also, when one is young, it's a comfort to feel that there are two of you against the world," says Alice, a copywriter. But she adds, "This comfort is illusory and soon dispelled, but is awfully nice while it lasts."

Kate

A medical librarian in a Midwestern city, Kate lives alone, has one pet cat, and is active in church groups, adult education classes, and her neighborhood association. Though she would like to be dating, she finds it hard to seek out situations in which she could meet suitable men. "I'm not into singles bars, dating services, personal ads, and the like," Kate, who is 38, says.

Kate feels slightly pressured on occasion by her mother, other relatives, and married friends. She forgives them, for she believes that they are interested solely in her happiness.

"It isn't that they think marrying is the thing to do—it's just that my friends who are happily married wish the same for me. I usually don't mind when they bring up the subject—I appreciate their caring about me and my happiness," Kate says. "But their concern can also be depressing. Sometimes I feel my marriage situation is futile, and discussing it reminds me that I will probably never marry."

Kate reports that she discusses her relationships with her mother—"except sexual matters. Somehow I feel that by not telling her intimate details, I'm protecting her if I should be hurt. We are very sensitive to each other's pain, and I don't want to inflict any of my disappointments on her."

Kate's mother is apparently highly supportive. "I think my mother would like to see me married, but she is also sure that I am and will be happy, whether or not I'm married," this daughter says.

4

Hopes

"I only want
her to
be happy!"

"Suppose when I grow up I can't get a husband," Molly asked her mother one day. "What will I do?"

"Don't worry," her mother soothed. "I'll get one for you."

Molly is six years old. Her mother is in her late thirties.

This mother's attempt to allay her daughter's anxiety comes somewhat as a surprise from a woman of today. What does she want and expect of Molly? Does she want her daughter merely to duplicate her own life?

Unquestionably, an opportunity was lost here with young Molly. Here was a chance to implant an encouraging message that marriage is not the only course that a woman's life can follow. Molly has already internalized the assumption that a husband will be necessary not only for her happiness but also to define her value as a woman. By confirming a traditional view that limits a woman's growth and power, Molly's mother has unwittingly compressed her daughter's expectations into a single goal—marriage—as the answer to future happiness. Molly will probably enter adulthood confident in the belief that marriage will automatically happen for her. And she will probably be deeply unhappy if this fairy tale scenario doesn't come true.

Is this where it starts? Will those brave and independent daughters who answered the questionnaires for this book adopt a double standard when they have daughters of their own? Will they begin to sound like *their* mothers?

Happiness and Marriage

Both the mothers' and the daughters' surveys opened with seven identical statements dealing with assumptions about the necessary ingredients for happiness and marriage. In responding, the women could indicate that they "agree strongly," "somewhat agree," are "not sure," "disagree somewhat," or "disagree strongly." (See **Appendices A and B**.)

a. "In order to be happy and fulfilled in her life, a woman must be married."

Both the mothers and daughters generally disagreed with that statement. One mother, who wasn't sure, added, "Most of my young single friends wish they were married."

b. "Success at a career is not as important for a woman as it is for a man."

Nearly all of the daughters and most of the mothers rejected that statement. Over the last 15 years, studies have shown women to believe that their own careers are equally as important as those of their husbands. These studies also indicate that work has become a more important component in the lives of women, both single and married, than it was just a generation ago. These mothers generally seemed to be aware of this.

c. "Friends and an active social life are just as crucial to a woman's happiness and well-being as a spouse."

Virtually all daughters and most mothers agreed with that.

However, Grace, a Boston psychotherapist who is the mother of an unmarried 27-year-old, added: "Ironically, there may be more factors today that make marriage more attractive than ever. Professional life has become more difficult, more demanding, less rewarding just as women have gained more access to it. Our children will have less and less control over their careers, and there is a breakdown in community life.

"Therefore, they will depend more on close friendship for continuity and a sense of belonging. It may become more important than ever that this include intimacy over a stretch of time with someone with whom one has a strong sexual bond, an ease of companionship, and the shared experience of raising a child or two. These factors may make marriage more important for happiness than friends and an active social life."

Her observations echo to what another mother said earlier about the comfort of being in a mutually supportive relationship against a sometimes harsh world.

Another relatively new factor that may serve to upgrade the desirability of marriage is the fear of AIDS. Having a single, steady, sexual partner who is known to be healthy may be one more vote in marriage's favor.

d. "A woman with young children should not work outside the home."

Most of the daughters and approximately one-half of the mothers disagreed. The younger women recognize that the sheer expense of raising families in today's economy make working outside the home less of an option and more of a necessity for themselves and their peers. Half the mothers surveyed for this book *did* work outside the home—at least part time—when their children were young, which accounts for their unexpectedly high response.

Grace disagreed strongly with the statement and had something provocative to add: "Ideally, both parents should be available to spend a lot of time with children when they are young. It is ridiculous that corporations cannot find some way to make this possible—with flexible time, shared jobs, or time off."

Another mother stated, "When my children were young, I felt strongly, as I do now, that a woman should be economically able to provide for her family and herself."

e. "Women should not have children outside of marriage."

Daughters and mothers parted company sharply on that statement. Most of the daughters endorsed single motherhood; most mothers did not.

Grace, while not necessarily condemning having children out-of-wedlock on moral grounds, offered some cautionary qualifications. "If the woman is well off, and has a closely knit circle of friends or an extended family who will stick around, [motherhood without marriage] might work perfectly well. But to try to raise a child totally on your own, working a 60-hour week to do it, with no time for friends or for yourself, would be exhausting. You'd probably either come to resent the child or build up such a dependency that the child would have difficulty making a break for independence later on. It's something to think about long and hard beforehand."

f. "A woman should take her husband's name when she marries."

There was a major disparity between daughters and mothers on that statement also; most of the daughters rejected the custom of using husbands' surnames, whereas most of the mothers stuck to it.

g. "Young women today are more selfish than other generations were."

Half of the mothers agreed with that statement, though one added, "Do you mean less willing to compromise? If so, then so are men—look at the divorce rate."

Somewhat less than half of the daughters bought the selfishness premise. One made an astute point: "I would prefer a less pejorative description. Young woman today are more focused on their *self-hood*."

Amy (profiled in Chapter 1) added: "We're willing to be 'selfish' enough to acknowledge, meet, and enjoy our own needs."

An analysis of the replies suggests that mothers and daughters tend to agree with each other more on abstract subjects—that women need not be married to be happy, that success in a career is an important concern, that friends are an important support group. It also suggests that unmarried women may have different expectations of marriage than their mothers have—thus, the disagreement on traditional norms of marriage itself, such as taking husbands' names, holding jobs when there are young children at home, and having children outside of marriage.

When women today say they wish to be married, they rarely desire the types of marriages their mothers had. Traditional marriages, in which men are the breadwinners and women housewives, are declining rapidly—but not solely for economic reasons. Women, far from gaining the happily-ever-after security and fulfillment they'd assumed would be theirs, began to realize that this type of marriage was often disappointing and frustrating, psychologically destructive to personal growth and self-esteem.

A small sample of the surveyed mothers were contacted by telephone and asked if they felt that the expectations of today's young men and women were different from those of their generation. Most agreed that they were. "For one thing, it's expected today that both partners will contribute to the family's economic base," said Rhoda, the mother who's a social worker. "The wife is not expected to just stay home; it's assumed she will have a career or job of her own."

Several mothers were ambivalent as to whether the different expectations would help or hinder a woman's chances for marriage, or the success of a marriage once entered into. "Women aren't willing to give up their careers, and men, even if intellectually they can accept this, have problems with it emotionally," said Virginia, a retired newspaper editor. "A man may be very pleased that his wife is working toward her Ph.D., but he still wants supper on the table and his shirts ironed.

"The other side of the coin is that women are no longer willing to accept men who just earn a living but won't share in the housework or child care. It's not so comfortable for men these days."

While all the mothers mentioned the increase in shared household and financial responsibilities, a few believed there is a decreasing level of commitment on the part of husbands and wives, and certainly the divorce rates would seem to back up this observation. Conversely, one mother felt that the partners in today's marriages expected too much of each other—"Marriage isn't easy. It's like a job," added June, a teacher. Only one mother indicated that she thought young men and women today approached marriage more realistically than in her day—"They're better educated and not inclined to think it's like the old movies where the couple rode off into the sunset and lived happily ever after."

Alternative Relationships

There is one other type of "marriage" that deserves mention here: the committed, longterm lesbian relationship. Different from both heterosexual love and female friendship, it nevertheless represents an alternative source of happiness for a sizable subgroup. The hopes and expectations of the lesbians who responded to the survey for this book were much like those of the heterosexual women. This kind of relationship is almost impossible for mothers to identify with, and many mothers of lesbians cannot acknowledge or accept it. Nevertheless, several mothers surveyed apparently can, and spoke of wanting their daughters' happiness above all else.

Gail

A systems analyst for a large firm, Gail is 37 years old and lives with her two cats and a dog—"I don't consider that I live alone," she says. "My pets are real friends." She is active in church and volunteer work.

Gail is a lesbian and was in a committed relationship for several years, but says that while she was very involved in gay rights, her lover was extremely closeted and terrified of being identified as gay, so the relationship did not endure. She would like to be dating (a woman) again, and believes 10 to 15 percent of the female population is homosexually oriented. She has both lesbian and non-gay friends.

Gail first became aware of her sexual preference while she was in high school—"I hadn't come out yet, but I knew my real story anyhow." She turned down a proposal of marriage from a man. Though she also, later, rejected an involvement offered by a woman, today she would like to be settled in a long-term committed relationship and hopes the time will come when gay relationships can be sanctified by marriage.

Gail's parents, apparently happily married, have four other children, also several grandchildren. Her mother leads an active life in many community projects. Both parents are aware of their daughter's homosexuality and are supportive and understanding, and Gail seems to value them as true friends.

"We know she would like to be in the right relationship with the right woman," they say. "We have superb rapport, and she knows that all we want for her is the happiness she wants for herself."

Husbands

Another part of the survey investigated mothers' and daughters' attitudes toward personality or behavioral traits in a man that would make him undesirable as a husband. An identical list of characteristics was included in both the mothers' and daughters' surveys. Each daughter was asked to check the characteristics in a man that would make it impossible for her to consider marrying him. The mother was asked to check those traits that she would not want in a husband for her daughter. (See **Appendices A and B**.)

On many character traits, mothers and daughters generally agreed. Both would overwhelmingly reject a potential spouse or son-in-law who disliked the daughter's friends and family or who was less intelligent than she. As well, a man was undesirable if he was sexually unfulfilling, refused to participate in household chores, and would insist that his wife not work outside the home after marriage. Since most of the mothers tended to regard their own marriages as fairly egalitarian—both partners were equal in making decisions—and because many of the mothers themselves were employed, it's not surprising that they would not want to see their daughters married to selfish, dictatorial men.

On the subject of household chores, daughters who would disqualify potential husbands who refused to help probably do so for different reasons than their mothers. The mothers remember well that when their children were young, and they were working, they did not expect or receive much household help from their mates. They want their daughters to be less burdened. The daughters, however, may regard sharing housework and child care with their future husbands as a given, and they take it for granted that this will happen.

Generally, men today do participate in home chores and child care more than their fathers and grandfathers did, but all the current research on this subject reveals that most are still only marginally helpful. Study after study has shown that even when women hold outside employment for the same number of hours that their husbands do, they nevertheless continue to shoulder the major burdens of housework and rearing children. As one working wife and mother complained, "I want to be the helper for a change."

In her book, *A Lesser Life*, Sylvia Ann Hewlett writes that one reason for the disparity between wives and husbands in terms of housework is that women still earn considerably less than men. It makes a certain economic sense for a family to put the husband's job first. If one partner is to leave the work force to raise a child, or to stay home when a child is ill, it will cost less for the lower-earning parent to do it.

But by interrupting her career, the wife lowers her promotion possibilities and earning potential. Thus, Hewlett points out, women do the housework because they earn less, and they earn less because they are also doing the housework.

Some women, aware of the unequal situation they are likely to find themselves in, count on the combined salaries to pay for a housekeeper, a not unrealistic solution. While they will probably have to assume the primary responsibility for keeping the household running, they won't have to do all the actual work.

Hewlett quotes Simone de Beauvoir writing thirty years ago: "Many young households give the impression of being on a basis of perfect equality. But as long as the man retains economic responsibility for the couple, this is only an illusion."

Many husbands tend to dismiss their wives' earnings as discretionary despite the fact that this contribution to the household is usually essential—and may in fact be equal to their own. According to the U.S. Census Bureau, 34 percent of wives in couples age 25 to 34 earn more than their husbands—hardly a negligible part of the family income. (And 25 percent of wives in age groups 35 to 44 outearn their husbands; in ages 45 to 54, 18 percent do so.)

Further, even if the husband is unemployed and his wife is working a 40-hour week to support the family, she still does most of the housework.

Only one-fourth to one-third of mothers and daughters would reject a man who was physically unattractive. A few mothers and daughters objected to a man of a different race and regarded a mixed-marriage possibility as out of the question.

However, mothers and daughters had very different concerns on several other traits. Mothers were more likely to insist that potential husbands for their daughters not be of a different religion or unable to have children. They also ruled out men who were more than five years younger, earned less, or had a lower education than their daughters.

The daughters were much more concerned than their mothers about similar political beliefs; nearly 40 percent indicated that they would find different politics a problem in a potential husband. Today's younger women seem to recognize that a political philosophy is reflective of a person's value system and world view, and therefore fundamentally significant. Their mothers, on the other hand, tend to regard a political position as relatively unimportant in interpersonal relationships.

Most daughters indicated they would not reject men who earned less than they did, were less well educated, had a different religion, or couldn't have children. On the subject of religion, one woman reported that she was atheist or agnostic and therefore she felt that a man who had *any* religious beliefs would be a problem as a husband for her. On the other hand, a Portland woman insisted that she could not consider a man who had not accepted Christ as his savior.

One open-minded young woman, while she checked "Sexually unfulfilling" as a quality she would not want in a husband, added "And would not learn!" Another equally optimistic woman added "And untrainable."

At the end of the list of negative qualities, a space was left for "Other." Differences between mothers, and daughters, values showed up here also. A few mothers made important additions—"Nonsupportive of her life goals"; "Would try to change her lifestyle"; "Rigid religiosity"; "Uninterested in the arts and social issues"; "Condescending attitude"; "Greatly different value system."

But daughters had a lot to say. Many added character traits such as "violent, abusive, alcoholic, cruel, childish, selfish, cold."

Some were even more explicit: "Boring!" "Smoked or did drugs." "Gambler." "Closed mind." "Untrustworthy." "Lack of sense of humor."

"Had very different values and interests," said a Denver woman.

"Angry at women or at the recent changes that give women more opportunities," added a New York woman.

One perceptive and very choosy 27-year-old checked most of the qualities on the list and appended, "Was not good at and excited by his work and couldn't find anything else."

And a New Jersey woman wrote, "Significant financial debt or great immaturity about financial matters. Uses any physical force in an argument."

It appears that most of the daughters are much more particular about the kind of men they would consider as potential husbands than their mothers are on their behalf.

The striking differences in values and perceptions about what matters most in a husband undoubtedly accounts for much of the misunderstanding between mothers and daughters. Clearly, mothers would prefer sons-in-law who are older, better educated, and would be good providers—in other words, men who follow the traditional pattern and who fit their image of what suitable husbands were like in their day. Given the shortage of available men who are older than their daughters, the high education level of their daughters, and today's economy in which two salaries are usually needed to support a couple, much less a family, in relative comfort, what the mothers are saying, in effect, is, "Get married—to someone who isn't out there!"

And indeed, why should the daughters be searching for partners who fit standards they consider largely irrelevant, rather than be faithful to their own standards? The bottom line is that while many of the surveyed women would like to marry, they are not ready to settle into relationships that they consider too much of a compromise.

Advice

One of the questions on the mothers' survey was: "About which of the following subjects do you give advice to your daughter?" The corresponding question on the daughters' survey was, "On which of the following subjects do you receive advice from your mother?" The subjects listed on both were: financial matters, careers, friends, love, education, and major purchases.

Most of the daughters and mothers had quite different opinions on this matter. They differed not only on the subjects but on whether or not advice is given at all.

Some mothers claimed they never give advice; others said they do give advice on several or all the subjects listed, but most of them qualified their statement with: "only when asked." They say:

"I try never to give advice."

"I don't offer advice unless I'm asked, and I don't seem to be asked much."

"I give advice on anything she seeks my opinion on, if I have something to offer."

"I give my opinions on all, advice on none." One mother was refreshingly frank: "If asked, I'll give advice about anything! If not asked, I try to keep my mouth shut. I don't always succeed."

And another took a philosophical position while establishing her own priorities: "Children have a right to run their lives without interference. I have enough to do to keep up with my husband and our own life."

Sometimes a mother can be put in a contradictory, no-win position. Say a daughter brings up a matter that concerns her—something she has done or is considering that affects her life. Just the fact that she raises the matter for discussion with her mother can quite naturally be interpreted by the mother as sending up a trial balloon. Without directly asking for advice, the younger woman seems to want it. (And indeed she might.)

But then, when her mother inevitably responds with her opinion, the daughter may pull back or resent her for offering advice.

Most of the daughters surveyed feel that their mothers do give them advice, if only on one or two matters. This does not necessarily mean that they resent it—only that they hear what their mothers are saying.

"My mother responds with advice on any topic I bring up," reports one daughter. "She does not volunteer advice." This daughter keeps in close touch with her mother, who lives in a different city. Her mother would be the first person she would call with good news.

"My mother always worked at her profession and she has financial savvy," says Gloria, a program producer at a radio station. "Therefore I always seek her advice on financial matters."

The mother of Laura, the anesthesiologist, indicated that she does not give any advice, that her daughter makes her own decisions. Laura concurred except in the matter of major purchases, which she checked.

It would be particularly hard for a mother who is worried about her daughter's chances of marrying not to give advice on seeking a husband. One of the questions on the mothers' survey asked, "Do you think your daughter should be doing more to find a suitable partner?"

Mothers seemed undecided. "I'm not sure I know how a person goes about doing that," one said.

"Yes—engaging in more activities that include more men than women," replied a New Jersey mother.

"Possibly, but she does have an active social life," said a California mother.

"No," answered another. "I think if she meets the right partner she will know it. I don't think you can search effectively for a suitable partner—you should just be yourself."

"Yes, but how can you direct someone who is independent?" asked a mother in Baltimore. "Her choices in men would never be mine."

"No," said a Portland mother. "It is her life and her business who or when or if she sees someone."

"Yes, but she shouldn't answer any of those ads in the personals columns," replied a New York mother. "They sound as if they were written by perverts!"

"No," stated one mother who is not worried about her daughter and, according to her daughter, does not pressure. "I feel that if the hunt were more important to her, she would make more effort to find the deer crossings."

In cases where daughters are living with or dating men who are known to their mothers, the mothers were asked how they felt about them. Replies were quite positive. One mother certainly had a good attitude: "He is making her happy." In other words, this mother was saying, never mind how I feel about him personally—if he makes my daughter happy, that's the important thing.

The mothers were asked on their survey whether or not they thought their daughters were too picky. A few mothers agreed; some were unsure. And some seemed indignant. "Yes, but why not?" one asked. "My daughter is sweet, lovely, pretty, and sensitive!"

"She has high standards for herself and expects the same of others," said another loyal mother.

"I hope she *is* picky and never feels pressured to marry," a Denver mother chimed in.

And from an Atlanta mother: "One can't be too picky or have too high standards for the people one dates!"

So much for pickiness, as far as the mothers surveyed for this book are concerned!

Both the mothers' and daughters' surveys presented a list of descriptive terms relating to character traits, and asked which ones the mother stressed and encouraged the daughter to be when she was growing up. The qualities on the list reflected current values: "ambitious, popular, athletic, intelligent, creative, assertive, pretty, and independent."

Most mothers and daughters agreed that independence, ambition, and intelligence were the traits most stressed. Perhaps they did not regard the choices as being exclusive of others.

"How can you encourage prettiness?" Rhoda wanted to know. "I think my daughter *is* pretty, and that opinion has been expressed to her." Admittedly, "prettiness" might be seen as something a woman is born with, rather than something that can be developed—but a mother can certainly encourage healthy self-care, fastidious grooming, and good taste in personal appearance.

A few mothers, however, were unhappy with the rather unfeeling, aggressive traits on the list and added some civilized qualities. "How about a category for companionable, sensitive, loyal, caring, and warm?" asked Grace, "something other than 'popular' that deals with relationships with other people?"

"Dependability and responsibility," added Virginia.

"To always be mindful of others' needs and to always try to help the poor or less fortunate," wrote a sympathetic mother.

One mother rejected the whole list. "None," she said. "We stressed honesty and cooperation."

Eleanor

Eleanor has been married for 35 years and is the mother of two married sons as well as an unmarried daughter. She had some college but did not finish—as she puts it, her husband "rescued" her in her sophomore year. Her views on marriage and careers are quite traditional.

She is proud of her accomplished 33-year-old daughter, an industrial designer, but worries sometimes about her chances of marrying. On her questionnaire, Eleanor's daughter says she feels pressured by her mother, but what hurts her the most is that when her two brothers tease her about being an "old maid," and imply that she is so unlovely that no man will marry her, her mother doesn't stand up for her but seems to tacitly agree. Yet, Eleanor herself writes that her daughter just hasn't found the right person yet.

Eleanor gives advice only when asked, she claims. Her daughter says she receives advice from her mother on career, friends, love, and major purchases—but does not say the advice is unsolicited.

The many traits she checked on the list of qualities she would not want in a son-in-law seem to indicate that Eleanor has a high opinion of her daughter and feels she deserves a very superior mate. Asked if she thinks her daughter should be doing more to find a suitable partner, this mother agrees, and says she sometimes tries to introduce her to people. "I only want her to be happy," she says.

It seems somewhat paradoxical that in spite of the high divorce rate, marriage continues to be so desired by the majority of American women—and presumably by men as well. Perhaps people believe that when such a partnership does work out, it is so gratifying, the rewards so great, that it is worth the risk. Hope springs eternal.

But while most of the women surveyed for this book would like to marry, as they say, "the right person," they do not consider themselves to be living in the desolate vacuum that so much of the popular media portrays. And many are content with their lives except when they feel pressured.

Therefore the question: Could the pressure on women to marry be a contributing factor in the high rate of divorce?

Possibly some women hasten to marry to escape the pressure, to fulfill the expectations of their families and of society in general—and then realize they have made a mistake. Dr. Hall states that she has known women in her practice who have married first and considered afterward whether they truly wish to be married to the men they have chosen, or whether they want to be married at all.

At least one scholarly paper on changing attitudes toward marriage suggests that a growing acceptance of single life may actually serve to *increase* marital happiness. Marital choices may be wiser, the authors argue, if they are motivated by positive rather than by negative considerations. If women choose to marry not because of the pressure they feel from family and society, or because they feel there is something wrong with them if they don't, they are less likely to compromise their true feelings.

It could be argued that mothers who pressure their daughters to marry might be quite unintentionally laying the ground for their future unhappiness. Perhaps they could instead help to increase their daughters' possibilities for happiness by reinforcing the concept that a good life can be developed and enjoyed in singleness, and by assuring their daughters that they are proud of them, whatever life state they are in.

Sheila

Though only 28, Sheila, a marketing director, expresses feeling considerable pressure from others and a strong desire of her own to marry. "I would like to settle down, have kids," she says. "I haven't met the right person yet, but I feel he must be out there somewhere." Asked if she expected to be working continuously for the next 15 years, Sheila said no, she plans to be married and the mother of at least two children. She seldom places her career aspirations ahead of romantic involvements.

She once headed off a proposal: "He wasn't right for me—I would rather be single." But sometimes the pressure she gets from her mother, father, other relatives, and married friends makes her feel they don't trust her judgment or choices.

"They act as if they feel sorry for me. They can't accept my current lifestyle, and they assume I must be terribly unhappy, living alone and working. They ask questions like, 'Did you meet anyone at the party last night?' or 'How was your date?'—which make me defensive and hostile and wish I had never told anyone I was going to a party or had a date," Sheila explains.

Sheila's mother holds traditional values and has never worked outside the home since she married. She says she worries sometimes about her unmarried daughter. She is aware that Sheila would like to be married and assumes she must frequently place her career ahead of her personal life and is possibly too picky or has too high standards for the people she dates.

"I accept where I am at the moment and make the best of it," says Sheila. "I resent the assumption that I'm too hard to please, or that it's not okay for me to be content on my own. Sometimes the pressure I seem to get from all sides shakes my belief that I will eventually marry—to the person who's right for me."

Sheila could use some support from family and friends.

5

Choices

"My career

is not

negotiable"

Joan tells of a friend who was very anxious to meet men. This friend worked mostly with women, was uncomfortable in bars or singles' clubs, and didn't have a church affiliation, so she hit on what she thought was a sure way to meet men: She joined an adult education class in carpentry at a local school.

To Joan's friend's dismay, she found the class had an enrollment of 30 women—and no men.

So just how do single women get to meet men?

Most of the women surveyed for this book, when asked that question, answered "through friends" or "at work." One woman mentioned dating a man she met in an elevator—"We just got to talking"; another meets men through a folk-dancing group. Only a handful mentioned meeting people through other channels: personal ads, church or synagogue, adult education courses, singles' organizations, family members, or bars or clubs. No more than four or five are, for example, like Joan's friend, taking adult education courses for the purpose of being where the guys are likely to be—as one mother termed it, at the "deer crossings." The responses held for both women who are dating and those who are not but wish they were.

So the question arises: If single women are as desperate to marry as they are sometimes depicted, or even as eager as some of them admit, how come they aren't exploring every possible avenue to meet men? According to their comments about pressure, they certainly get plenty of suggestions and encouragement from relatives and friends.

The results of the survey indicate that single women do not focus their lives on meeting men. The women apparently are happy to meet men to date through the normal channels of work or friendships, but are very selective, and are not actively husband-hunting.

Dating

Although some 60 percent of the women questioned for this book are dating to some degree, most of those who are not indicated that they wish they were. The responses seem to indicate that the women enjoy the company of men and miss it when they don't have it. Many were unhappy with the frequency of their dates: more than half said they date somewhat less frequently than they would like, and 20 percent date much less than they would like.

The major reason most respondents gave for not dating was that they have not met the right person. "I have a friend who says that unmarried women are the cream of the crop, while unmarried men are the bottom of the barrel," remarks Amy. Her friend's cynical observation may hit home especially among educated, high-achieving, independent women.

The majority of women who indicated that they are not interested in dating either live with lovers or are already involved in exclusive, longstanding relationships. Conversely, those who date a number of people are more satisfied with their social life than those who are currently not dating.

"I have a relationship with one person that includes sex and may perhaps lead to marriage," says a Denver woman. "But I have social contacts with other men. This is an arrangement I prefer and can handle emotionally."

"I have been dating one man exclusively for six months," says a 29-year-old, "but I don't expect the relationship to lead to marriage. I have a very busy life. I enjoy being single and expect to remain so."

An Atlanta woman of 39 has three current relationships, all of them longterm—from three to six years. She doesn't expect any of them to lead to marriage. "Two of my dating relationships are platonic," she says. "I like a variety of activities and enjoy them with different people."

And one East Coast woman says that she is involved with one man that she would like to marry, but so far, while he is aware of her feelings, he hasn't made up his mind. The fact that he lives in another state puts a burden on the relationship. So in the meantime, she reports, "I'm enjoying seeing someone else right now."

Some women have had previous unsatisfactory relationships and are content to be by themselves or to socialize with one or two close friends. "I'm tired!" says Lynn. "I've had three longterm relationships that were not satisfactory to me, finally, and were very painful to end. I'm just not interested in going through a fourth."

"In the past I've been hurt in love relationships," says another woman. "I'm afraid to take a chance and prefer to be alone at this time." While this woman says she is "alone," she does not indicate that she is lonely. She lives with a male roommate, her dog and two cats. Her mother, who lives in another state, thinks she is seeing someone. (Perhaps her mother believes the roommate is this person.)

One question on the survey asked: "Would you go out with someone if you did not think there was a good chance of developing a serious relationship with that person?" Few women made *a priori* judgments about the men they would date in terms of a potential relationship. Instead, it seems that most women enjoy male friendships and date sheerly for the pleasure of male company. They apparently can appreciate men who are not possible husbands, and they don't assume that a date has to be a prelude to marriage.

Daters Compared

There is a clear difference between women who date and those who don't, in terms of their focus on their careers. Asked on the survey whether they "never," "seldom," "occasionally," or "frequently" place their career aspirations ahead of their romantic involvements, the majority of non-daters said they do so occasionally or frequently. Many fewer women who are currently dating said they never or seldom put their careers ahead of dating.

Interestingly, women who are dating place themselves slightly higher on their career ladders than women who are not. Those women who are striving to move up in their careers seem to devote most of their attention to work, whereas women who feel they are well established in their careers or who have achieved most of their career goals may feel freer to relax and seek the companionship of men.

There is an element of choice among some of the women who are not dating. They are willingly giving up personal involvements, at least temporarily, for the sake of their careers.

Age as well seems to be a strong factor in whether or not women are dating. The older women in the sample for this book are much less likely to date than the younger women. A slight majority of those over 33 are not dating. Of the women under 33 years old, twice as many do date as those who don't.

Although being on the topside of 30 may be a detraction to dating for some of these women, high income is not. One might predict that men would be somewhat intimidated by high achievers, or at least by women who are pulling in good money by their own wit and energy. Yet, success does not relegate the women surveyed for this book to lonely nights. As it turned out, women with higher salaries were slightly more likely to date.

Another surprise appeared in the survey analysis regarding dating and non-dating women. Several questions were carefully aimed to determine attitudes toward marriage that might be considered either feminist or traditional. For our sample, a woman would be considered non-feminist if she tended to concentrate her energies less on her career and more on relationships. Professional studies have shown that many women do fear that feminist attitudes make them less desirable to men—even though they won't change their beliefs because of it. "I m afraid my independent attitude turns men off," admitted a woman surveyed for this book.

However, women of all ages who scored high on non-traditional attitudes in the questionnaire turned out to be more likely to be dating than women who scored medium or low. A partial explanation for this might be that non-traditional women are more likely to be open to dating men who are younger, earn less money, or are less educated than they. Or, possibly, a woman who has achieved high placement in her career and who is also involved with a man realizes that the relationship, while fulfilling, is not the only source of satisfaction in her life. Such a woman would therefore score high on the scale of feminist values.

Today, the whole subject of dating has to be seen against the ever-growing threat of AIDS. How do the risks of deadly infection affect single women? So far, the evidence is mixed. Some women are concerned but confused about the means by which the disease is transmitted. And many are apparently engaged in what AIDS educators would call high risk behavior, not regularly taking precautions to protect themselves in their sexual encounters. Part of the problem, they say, is resistance among men to using condoms, despite the fact that men as just as vulnerable as women.

But part of the problem is that some women simply think that AIDS is a kind of science fiction. Dr. Hall notes that she has encountered women who, if they think of AIDS at all, regard it as being somebody else's problem and thus take chances. Fortunately, she has also observed that AIDS has changed the sex habits of many more women. They are limiting their contacts. Fear of the disease in some cases, she says, serves to promote monogamy among couples and is influencing those in longterm relationships to stay together.

Some of the survey participants were asked, by telephone, how they think the AIDS epidemic has affected the sexual behavior of unmarried women. A few believe women have simply become fatalistic and haven't changed, but most think that women are becoming much more careful. "Recreational sex has decreased," said one woman. "And more and more women are carrying condoms and insisting that the men they are intimate with use them."

Men and Women's Careers

One of the most sensitive areas in the relationship between men and women is the degree of a woman's dedication to her career. Up to a point, a man's immersion in his work is considered admirable and understandable. A "go-getter" is admired for his ambition, and it is rare to find his behavior belittled on the grounds that he is a "workaholic." But as every ambitious, hard-working business or professional woman knows, she is likely to be regarded as a workaholic far sooner than her male colleague, at least in the eyes of the people in her personal life.

A woman may resent it when a man she is involved with becomes totally preoccupied with his work, and will often feel neglected when his career sharply curtails the time he can spend with her. However, a woman's tolerance is usually much higher than that of a man's in a reverse situation. As was noted earlier, women as part of their acculturation have been taught to defer to men's wishes, to be patient. Men, as part of their upbringing, are not prepared to be in romantic relationships with ambitious, dedicated career women. Many men are still uncomfortable in this situation because they feel their own role has been preempted.

Almost half the women surveyed report that men they have been involved with at one time or another have resented their devotion to their work. Most of these women admit that they frequently or occasionally had placed their careers ahead of their romantic involvements.

The men showed their resentment in various ways:

"One man I was dating used to telephone me at work and expect me to chat endlessly," says Emily, the editor mentioned in Chapter 1. "Often I was in a rush to meet a deadline and couldn't stay on the phone. He would get angry when I'd tell him I couldn't talk."

Barbara, a travel agent, says that a man she was seeing would become angry whenever her work kept her from being always available to him. "He'd get even more upset if I had to travel on business or take a trip without him," she adds.

"A man I was involved with was constantly interrupting me at work," states Gloria, the program producer at a radio station. "Also, he would often criticize working women and college-educated women in general."

Denise, the dress designer, reports: "Someone I went out with who was in a similar field did not acknowledge my expertise and felt he always had to talk professional jargon and blow his own horn to make himself appear more competent and knowledgeable than I was."

"When I dated a man who worked in the same field I do, he constantly tried to put down my job because it wasn't in the mainstream of the company's business," recalls Lynn. "Another insisted on telling me how to do my job, even though he never really tried to find out what my job was. I had to stop talking about work so I wouldn't have to listen to him make a jerk of himself."

Other women report similar experiences when they talked about their work to men they were involved with:

"He would act jealous and become passive/aggressive."

"He would change the subject very abruptly to something totally unrelated to my work."

"He couldn't acknowledge that what I was doing was important or as demanding as what he did."

A nurse says a man she was living with would frequently want to stay out late when she had to be at work by seven the next morning, or would accept invitations that he knew would conflict with her work schedule. And because his workday was different from hers, he would often want her to stay home from her job just to be with him.

One business executive ended a relationship with a man because he made sarcastic remarks about "executive decisions" and became very domineering in social settings, especially among his colleagues.

And one woman who lived with her lover says that his expressions of resentment and discomfort with her career involvement took the form of sexual intimidation—"colder, less frequent, rougher."

Those women in the sample for this book who are without satisfying relationships have not elected *not* to date—indeed they would like to be dating—but many are having trouble finding men who are comfortable with their career ambitions. Women currently not dating were more likely to have been in previous relationships with men who resented their dedication to work. No doubt the unpleasantness of these experiences has made non-dating women considerably more selective.

There may also be an element of denial among some women who are dating or involved in relationships. They may unconsciously close their eyes to the signs of discomfort or disapproval about their work habits and career aspirations. Several indicated on the questionnaire that they were unsure if men they were involved with were uncomfortable when they talked about their work. In a peculiar form of accommodation, they refuse to accept that the men they admire and love might be threatened by their ambition and success. These women make excuses for their men's lack of understanding and support, and for the encouragement they would like to be able to count on.

Beth

A 32-year-old veterinarian in a Western city, Beth says she was formerly involved with a man who very definitely resented the amount of time her work demanded—"We had many arguments over my schedule and patient load."

Now she dates a number of people, and thinks one of

her relationships might lead to marriage eventually, but at this point she does not feel like making a commitment.

Beth is active in several professional organizations, and also does a fair amount of community work. Her five best friends are women. She owns her own home, lives alone with her two dogs and a cat. If she received a professional honor or had some special recognition for work she had done, the first person she would tell would be one of her best friends—but she says that when she told her mother, she knows her mother would be delighted and supportive.

"Though I think my mother would be happy if I married, and I know she would want me never to be lonely, she doesn't pressure me about marriage," Beth says. "I don't talk to her very often about my romantic relationships except to mention them in passing. Do I think she'd like to hear more? I'm not sure." (Her mother indicates that she does worry about her daughter marrying, and confirms that they rarely discuss her love life, but she is confident that when Beth does become seriously involved, she'll hear about it.)

Beth's parents are happily married. "I like the way they interact and delight each other," she says. "If I ever did decide on a permanent relationship, theirs is the kind I'd like to have."

Asked if she had assumed that she would be married by her present age, Beth says yes, and that she had never questioned the storybook fantasy about her prince coming along on a white horse. But now, she realizes that "Marriage involves a lifelong struggle between two people who start off being socialized and acculturated *very* differently."

She acknowledges the differences in attitude between men and women regarding the other's preoccupation with career. She observes that women are still expected to make adjustments for the careers of their husbands far more than the other way around.

Beth's mother says her daughter is comfortable being single and seems to feel it is perfectly natural. "She is very career-oriented," she says. And indeed, this daughter, in her survey, radiates confidence and life satisfaction.

Proposals

The notion that single women are pining away for a chance to get married, or have never been asked, does not hold true for the sample in the survey. Approximately three-quarters of them have either rejected outright offers of marriage or, anticipating proposals, have acted in such a way as to thoroughly discourage them. Furthermore, very few, years later, seem to have regrets.

Asked their reasons for rejecting or deflecting those proposals, most women simply replied that they didn't love the men who had asked them, or that they knew they wouldn't be happy with them. A few felt they were too young at the time.

Some women were more explicit. "I don't think the man truly valued me as a person," said one. "I think he wanted to get married for his own reasons that had nothing to do with me. He had a 'grand plan' that he needed a wife to fit into."

"I don't think I really want to be married," stated Lynn, "although an amazing number of people try to convince me I don't really mean it. It seems to bend people's minds out of shape when I say it, but the one time I did, even though the man I was talking to assumed I didn't mean it, I felt more honest having said it flat outright."

Women are apparently so conditioned to assume they will marry as a matter of course, and to automatically want to marry, that those who truly don't are forced to question themselves about being "normal." While most women do wish to marry for any one or combination of reasons, some apparently do not—again for a combination of reasons. But the pressure of society is so strong that they have a hard time coming to terms with their true feelings.

It appears from the analysis of the surveys that to a large extent, many of the women have chosen not to be married. This does not mean they are against marrying; a sizable number express a desire to be married. But they qualify their wishes with statements to the effect that they want marriages in which they are equal partners. They are not about to marry just for the sake of acquiring the status of wife.

There is some evidence in the sociological literature that suggests that while marriage is still a desirable event for many women, it may be less attractive now than previously. This may be true especially for educated, professional women. It does not mean that all professional women who are unmarried are completely satisfied with their lives (although many are), but that the costs associated with being married are too high.

Among many social scientists studying women and career priorities, Mary C. Regan and Helen E. Roland, writing in the *Journal of Marriage and the Family*, observed that women are still expected to fit their own careers around childrearing and their husbands' career needs. Sensing this, ambitious women may decide to postpone marriage in favor of dedication to their own careers—and as some demographics show, postponement could mean never.

Studies of women in high-pressure professions or executive positions have repeatedly shown that the majority of them tend to be single—not because they are unattractive, or anti-marriage, but because they are often too busy to put themselves in a position to meet men, or because they realize that they would not be able to manage their careers within the framework of a traditional marriage. And among women on the fast track, if they are married, fewer still have children. While successful men almost without exception have the benefit of supportive wives, families, and undemanding home environments, which help make their achievements possible, few women can count on this—and usually find "having it all" takes a great toll. Divorce rates are higher than normal within this group of women.

Rachel

A 27-year-old graduate student in music, Rachel shares a house with her lover and several other people.

Her commitment to her music is strong, and she frequently puts it ahead of her involvement with her lover, who tries to be supportive, she says, but wishes he could have more of her time. Rachel frequently asks him not to disturb her when she's practicing.

"My career is not negotiable," Rachel says. "If, for example, I had a chance to study at a conservatory in another state, I'd move whether he came along or not."

Her previous lover, who was well launched on a successful career of his own, was happy with her when she was an undergraduate student, but became increasingly uncomfortable when she talked about her own goals in music.

Rachel reports that several past lovers would probably have gotten married if she had wanted to, but she was vehemently opposed. She is not sure if she would want to marry her current lover either. She gets a certain amount of pressure from relatives.

"People seem very curious about my ambivalence toward marriage, and in fact, I get the impression that some of my relatives and friends don't want to hear about it," Rachel says. "Some family members assume I want my present relationship to lead to marriage, and don't know how to take it when I tell them I'm uncertain whether I want to marry at all. But people who know me well leave me alone.

"Marriage seems to work really well for some people, but I'm not sure it would for me," she confesses. "Perhaps I'll change my negative feelings in time, though some of the doubts I had ten years ago are still with me."

Coping with Pressure

While most of the women surveyed have certainly exercised, consciously or otherwise, a great deal of choice in remaining single—by frequently putting their energies and time into their careers instead of concentrating on relationships that could lead to marriage, and by being extremely selective—they still have to cope with pressure to marry.

Not all of them experience the pain, depression, and feelings of hopelessness that some described in Chapter 1. Some are merely vaguely annoyed, others seem to be able to handle the pressure without becoming overanxious. In other contexts, psychologists have pointed out that people can, to a certain extent, exercise some choice and control over their feelings by their behavior. Just as behavior follows feelings, feelings can be affected by behavior: If a person doesn't feel a certain way, but acts as though he or she does, the appropriate emotion will follow. Some women may employ this tactic in coping with pressure. By acting as though they don't mind, after a while they find that they mind much less.

Sharon is an attorney and at 35 feels considerable pressure—not so much from her mother as from other relatives, friends, colleagues. "I'm frequently questioned about whether I want children and advised that I should try marriage at least once," she says. (The "at least once" bears out Nancy's observation, in Chapter 1, that today, a divorced woman is completely accepted, while a woman who has never married is stigmatized the way a divorced woman was in the past.)

Sharon reacts coolly. "I point out that what is available in marriage can be obtained by being single as well. Sex is available, children are available, success and financial comfort are available. Presently I'm doing well as a single lady."

A 30-year-old New York woman states, "I have twelve cousins, and I'm the only unmarried female. Some of my relatives make comments that I will soon be over the hill. I ignore it. I'm happy with my life the way it is."

This woman says she talks to her mother on the telephone every day, keeps her up-to-date on her life. Her mother does not pressure her about marriage; this mother/daughter relationship seems to be an example of the analysis' finding that a mother who feels in touch with her daughter is less likely to worry about the fact that her daughter is unmarried.

A St. Louis woman, 39 years old, is pressured by relatives. "They ask, Why aren't I married? Do I ever expect to marry? Don't I want children? That's what I hear every time there's a family gathering," she reports. "Some of them even tell me all the things I'm missing by not being married. Depending on who the person is, I may politely give a brief answer without elaborating, or I may change the subject without answering, or I sometimes say flat out that I don't want to discuss the subject. It doesn't bother me much any more."

A 30-year-old Denver woman is also able to stand up to the pressure she gets from relatives. "I ignore it," she states. "I am very happy with my life."

Some women indicate that they shrug off pressure with jokes. "I tell them that my wedding will be on the same day as the Pope's," says a Portland woman.

Others try to answer directly, honestly, and completely. "I explain exactly why I have made the choice not to marry at this time," an Atlanta woman writes.

A 37-year-old who is both working and going to graduate school reports getting pressure from all sides—from mother, other relatives, co-workers. "I'm teased about being an old maid. There's verbal speculation about my sexual preferences. And though a few of my male colleagues gripe about their marriages and advise me never to marry, most of my co-workers feel compelled to tell me stories of wedded bliss.

"When I was younger, I used to become angry," she says. "But now that I've developed a stronger sense of self, I can usually ignore pressure."

Jackie

This 31-year-old buyer for a department store lives at home with her parents, but while they live under the same roof and care about each other, similarities seem to end there. They share very few viewpoints. Jackie is a free spirit, hopes to make a career change, likes sports, has many interests, dates a number of people, and has no wish to settle down. Her mother is a very traditional and domestic woman who does not envy the career opportunities young women have today; she worries about the fact that her daughter is not married.

Jackie says that while her mother is supportive of her career plans and hopes, she knows her mother feels the life she is currently leading is crazy and unsettled.

"She strongly believes that the only right way to live is to be married," says Jackie. "But I've always wanted a different kind of life. I never assumed that I would grow up and get married, with a big wedding and all that sort of thing. I've always been involved in dancing and sports, and my goals have centered on them.

"Besides, I have a very poor image of marriage. I think it causes people to lose their individuality and freedom. I know of very few marriages among my friends that I respect and envy. If I fell so much in love that I decided to get married, I would try to make it work. But right now I don't want to be committed too heavily in any one relationship—I value my freedom too much. Dating several people as I do affords me the space I need."

Asked if she has ever turned down a proposal of marriage, she says she has, and that she doesn't regret it—though "maybe later in life I will." She is also careful to deflect any possible proposals. "I feel strong enough about not wanting to get married at this point that I let it be known right away. It clears the air." She rarely talks to her mother about her relationships except to mention them in passing.

Jackie feels pressure about marriage not only from her mother but from her married friends and sometimes from relatives. "At times, this pressure bothers me and makes me wonder if I'm right or wrong in my feelings and lifestyle. But usually I stand up for my beliefs."

6

Partnership

"I won't

settle for

less"

It is now ten years since Nancy Friday's book, *My Mother, My Self, The Daughter's Search for Identity,* was published. It was a personal and extensive examination of the mother/daughter relationship as it was perceived then by a woman who had reached adulthood perhaps ten or fifteen years earlier. "The fear of freedom," she wrote, "which we dress up and call the need for security, is rooted in the unresolved half of us which is still a child, still looking for a man to replace the mother we never successfully left. So long as we have our need for symbiosis, we will not believe we can make it on our own."

Much has changed since those words were written. Women have discovered they can indeed make it on their own. Economic security is no longer the tantamount reason for a woman to marry. Living patterns have shifted: young people leave the parental nest sooner to face the responsibilities of living on their own. While the need for parental approval seems still very much alive in many of the women who participated in the survey for this book, the need for symbiosis is no longer an appropriate way of defining the relationship of daughters with their mothers.

Parents' Marriages

Nancy Friday took the position that women regard their mothers' lives as the model for their own relationships with men, particularly in terms of how they perceived their mothers' married life with their fathers. "We want to believe that life with father is as nice as mother says, but in our heart we know it just isn't so," she wrote.

Although the issue of how the unmarried daughters perceived

their parents' marriage was not addressed in the survey for this book, some women were approached later by telephone and asked if and how their views of marriage were colored by their observations of their parents' married life. Of the 15 women chosen, all but three agreed that their parents' marriages had a major impact on how they thought about marriage for themselves. Only four were the daughters of divorced mothers. Three had mothers who weren't sure they would marry the same spouse again; four of the mothers were sure they would.

Not all reports were critical. "I tend to think of my parents' marriage as boring and I would like mine to be more exciting," said Laura. "But they get along well, and their marriage shows me that two people can be comfortable together for a long time."

Both Beth and Amy, you may recall, were encouraged by their parents' marriages. And an Atlanta woman wrote on her questionnaire that her parents' marriage had seemed fairly easy—she had come to respect it greatly as she realized the challenge of staying together.

But when one considers that out of the sample, two-thirds of the women took a dim view of their parents' marriage and said they wanted to avoid making the same mistakes as their parents, such reports suggest that most of the women surveyed would not want for themselves the kind of marriages their parents had.

"I don't want to repeat what I saw in my parents' marriage," said a St. Louis woman. "It had a very negative effect on me."

"My mother was financially dependent on my father," reported a Philadelphia women. "If she had ever wanted to leave him, she couldn't have supported herself. This made me see the need to be very independent and able to take care of myself."

"My parents' marriage was unhappy," said Mary, the 40-year-old television executive mentioned in Chapter 1. "It certainly had an influence on me—I ran away from all marriage possibilities."

"I could never subjugate myself to a man the way my mother did to my father," Lynn stated. "I didn't really get to know my mother until after my father died."

Jenny also had a negative view. "My parents were incompatible and had unrealistic expectations of each other," she said. "I think people need to really know themselves and be comfortable with themselves before they marry. I would certainly think long and hard about myself and the man before I would marry."

"I decided long ago I wasn't going to make their mistakes," added Barbara. "Their marriage is certainly a factor in the reasons I am not married."

Fewer Marriages

Previous researchers have noted that setting up an independent home, either alone or with roommates, can lead young people to develop tastes and skills that reduce their orientation to exclusively family roles. It seems unlikely, however, that being able to support oneself, and create a home of one's own, in themselves would account for the lowered marriage rate among young women today. To examine this, the survey put the question to both mothers and daughters: Why do you think fewer young professional women are marrying these days?

To answer that question, there were eight reasons to choose from: "Too high standards," "[the women's] high status intimidates men," "shortage of men," "enjoying independence," "careers taking up their time," "too old," "men too demanding in what they expect women to give up for marriage," and "other." (See **Appendices A and B**.)

Over 70 percent of the women, both mothers and daughters, who answered the question indicated that they believe one reason fewer professional women are marrying is that they enjoy the independence that living alone affords them. They begin to take for granted the freedom that the single lifestyle allows.

Mothers and daughters alike also thought that a professional woman's status is often intimidating to men. The responses given by many of the daughters in Chapter 5 sketched the ways that men showed their discomfort with the success of women in their careers.

"Women are responding quicker than men are to role changes and new definitions," observed a New York daughter.

A 27-year-old woman states, "Younger men—my contemporaries—are frightened by intelligent women who have the potential to earn more than they and to succeed at whatever they choose."

Denise's comment suggests a similar view: "Women have outdistanced men in their emotional maturity and will accept less sex-role stereotyping from men since they can take care of themselves."

Quite a few women expressed the opinion that there is less need, economic or otherwise, for them to marry. "Professional women don't see the emotional or economic reason for marriage," comments Jenny, who owns a public relations agency. "They don't need marriage to validate themselves as full people."

"A woman with a full life, the ability to support herself, and access to a sexual relationship has as little inducement to marry as a man does," writes Linda, the biochemist who spoke in Chapter 1. "Even if she has no family close by, friends—especially other women—can create a family for her and give her emotional support."

Another woman agrees, stating tersely, "Women don't need marriage for status or money."

One self-confident 28-year-old put it this way: "Professional women realize that marriage is not necessary for ultimate happiness and total life fulfillment."

A Portland women checked *all* the reasons on the list and added that she thought one more reason some women might not marry is that they are lesbians. (She revealed later in the questionnaire that she is a lesbian.) There are apparently no reliable demographic statistics on gay men and women. It is estimated that there are three times as many homosexual men as gay women, though lesbians may simply be more closeted. The numbers of homosexual men are sometimes cited as a contributing factor in the marriage squeeze. "For every male homosexual couple, that means two fewer marriageable men," a mother remarked.

High standards were weighted more heavily by mothers than daughters as an obstacle to establishing relationships with men. Yet, mothers showed a certain ambivalence about their daughters standards. Asked later in the questionnaire if they thought their daughters were too picky, few mothers did—and some said, in effect, that their daughters were superior people and had a right to be choosy.

Grace, the psychotherapist, believes there's a shortage of men who can meet the standards of today's young professional women. "Better keep the standards and give up the men," was her advice on the subject.

Paradoxically, while somewhat fewer daughters checked "too high standards for prospective husband," their selectivity showed up in other responses, as in the qualities they would expect in a husband, and in their insistence on equality in the marriage relationship.

As a Denver woman sums up: "Women today have a fear of dependence. They are skeptical about the institution of marriage as it functioned in the past, and they have less social and material need for marriage. All this makes them more selective of men—and there seems to be a shortage of good men."

Mothers also mentioned their daughters' devotion to their work as a contributing factor in the lower marriage rates of young professional women. "They want to be loved as they are, not just for sex, and they don't want to give up their careers," stated one sympathetic mother.

An Atlanta daughter stated, "Many professional women are just delaying marriage until their careers are firmly established." But one mother observed that by the time professional women have become well established in their careers, there are minimal opportunities for them to meet interesting single men socially.

Surprisingly, fewer than half of either mothers or daughters believe the man shortage is a reason. Daughters born between 1952 and 1957, however, are more likely than others to be aware that one exists. One woman had this to say: "Men who are unmarried don't seem to want a committed relationship. They're aware that there are more single women than men, and they like to take advantage of it."

In follow-up telephone interviews, several mothers were asked if they were aware that there is, in their daughters' generation, an actual shortage of males. None of the mothers thought that there was. Many, like Grace, believe that there is a shortage of *desirable* men, but not an actual numerical shortage. However, as explained earlier, thanks to the baby boom of the 1950s there are many more women and men who are currently between their late 20's and late 30's than there are people who were born just ahead of them. Since women tend to marry men slightly older than themselves, and since men generally prefer to marry women slightly younger, there are fewer unmarried men available to the unmarried women in the age group surveyed for this book.

This fact alone does not explain why fewer professional women are marrying. But it is interesting that this reason was not highlighted as a crucial factor by the women surveyed here.

A few mothers and daughters mentioned that the current high rate of divorces and the number of unhappy marriages have made women very cautious about marrying. Add those sociological factors to personal negative experiences—"Women who have been hurt deeply before are afraid of intimacy," said one daughter—and marriage becomes something that must be weighed carefully.

Change of Heart

The survey for this book bore out many other studies in ascertaining that women's degree of commitment to their careers has risen sharply in the last few decades. In this respect the women differ from their mothers and from most other women of previous generations. Moreover, their views of marriage have changed even from their own expectations.

"When you were 18, did you think you would be married by your current age?" asked the survey. "Do you think your feelings about marriage have changed since that time, and if so, how have they changed?"

Two-thirds of the women said that at 18, they had expected to be married by their current ages. And about the same proportion had radically changed their feelings about marriage. Most of them remember having fairy-tale notions about marriage; they assumed that a husband, a large house, and children would come automatically right after college. Now, they feel they are much more realistic, and when they speak of marriage, they speak of partnership.

Barbara: "I know I'd be unhappy with anything less than a 50-50 relationship, and I won't settle for less. I'm interested in meeting my own needs, not just a man's."

Sharon: "I no longer expect a knight in armor on a white horse, or in a Mercedes, to 'rescue' me and transform me. The man I marry must accept me as I am."

Jane: "I'm more realistic, less idealistic and romantic. Now I'm more desirous of an intimate friend, one who understands that we will both grow, individually and together."

Karen: "I'm not as tolerant or as willing to compromise as I was when I was 18. I've developed a life and a career that I enjoy. I'm not as easily in love as I was then; I consider the whole person. And I realize the hard work involved in maintaining a relationship."

Jennifer: "Love is not enough. Marriage is more like a partnership than a love affair. You have to have common goals and the motivation to try for them. Mutual respect and values are critical. You both have to be contributing partners to meeting each other's needs."

Christine: "I now realize it's not as simple as falling in love and having marriage and children fall neatly into place. There must be a lot of effort and give-and-take from both partners. There is a very practical side to marriage that I couldn't see at 18."

But some women, while more realistic now than they were at 18, feel their loss of romanticism and naivete has not deterred their wish to marry. They are not at all ambivalent on this point. And others who at 18 thought they would never want to marry have now decided that they do.

"At 18, I believed marriage happened whether you were looking for it or not, and that children came along more or less automatically, and that divorce was unthinkable," says Joan, who spoke in Chapter 1 of her misgivings about her six-year live-in relationship with her lover. "Now I believe that marriage is very special, something you practically luck into, though I also realize it takes a great deal of compromise to make it work. I feel I was very selective in choosing the man I'm involved with, and somewhere inside me I feel resentful that I'm not married. Yes, my feelings about marriage have changed—but I still want it sometime in my life."

"When I was 18, I thought marriage was a trap, and I couldn't imagine finding someone I'd want to spend my life with," writes a 33-year-old. "But now, I'm tired of being alone. Friends are wonderful, but in the final analysis, a significant other is very desirable."

A 29-year-old who lives with her lover writes, "I wasn't sure I would marry, and felt if I remained single, that would be okay too. Now I realize it's so much nicer to be with someone. I'm in no rush, but I can see being with my current man forever—marriage is not so far from my mind."

A 27-year-old New York woman has also changed in favor of marriage: "At 18, I felt I would never marry. Due to my parents' poor relationship, I had a very low opinion of marriage. But now I have enough confidence in myself to someday enter a permanent relationship without compromising myself or harboring resentment."

"Coming from a broken home, I understand the fragility of marriage and the effort involved in maintaining it," says a 26-year-old Denver woman. "I would not marry just for the sake of being married or just to have children. I want to spend the rest of my life with a man who can be my best friend, lover, and a good parent. I have very high standards, but I'm confident that someone will meet them."

And Nancy, the assistant D.A., says, "When I was 18 and even in my early to mid-20's, I had no real desire to be married or have children. I looked upon marriage as a loss of freedom and independence. Now, at 32, I would like to be settled and married and have a child. Career and job are important, but I think ultimately it's family, children, and people you love and who love you that give meaning to life."

Andrea

Thirty-one years old, black, and an obstetrician, Andrea has been dating one man exclusively for over three years. She thinks marriage is a strong possibility. In terms of her career goals, she considers herself at 5 on a scale of 1 to 7. Although she expects to continue to work if she marries, she would take time off to raise children.

In the past, she has been involved with men who resented her career, and in at least one relationship she made it clear that she was not interested in marrying. "He was too immature," she says.

Asked what qualities would make a man unlikely as a potential husband, she indicated that if he earned significantly less money and had lower intelligence and education than she, he would be a problem for her. She felt strongly that different political beliefs and a dislike of her friends and family would also be a deterrent. She would reject anyone with an alcohol or drug problem, as well as anyone with mental illness. But if he refused to do household chores, that doesn't matter to Andrea. Perhaps she envisions hiring household help.

When she was 18, she assumed she would be married

by her present age. Now, though she no longer feels marriage is her ultimate goal, she would certainly consider it. She would want a marriage in which she and her husband were able to communicate fully. "And we should be able to have fun together," she adds.

Andrea feels pressure to marry from her mother, married friends, and co-workers. "Everybody points out how long Peter and I have been going out together," she says. "I just act noncommittal. Sometimes I just say maybe we will marry. Or I may say Peter doesn't believe in marriage, or some such."

In spite of Andrea's high-status profession, she thinks her mother believes that she is rejecting her position as wife and mother by not marrying. "In my mother's eyes, marriage is a better measure of a woman's success than a good career is," says Andrea.

She has always told her mother about her relationships, but never negative information. "She wouldn't understand and would criticize," says Andrea.

Asked what she thought her mother's reaction would be to good news about a promotion or honor she received, Andrea thinks her mother would be somewhat reluctantly proud. "She would congratulate me, but in a rather subdued way," says this accomplished woman.

Having It All

In the early days of "women's lib," say 20 years ago, ambitious, educated women fought to prove their equal abilities in fields and professions previously dominated by men. They capitalized on the gains made by the few courageous and dedicated women who had opened the way, and made inroads that other women could follow. And then, because most husbands did not rush to take up the slack at home, these career women found themselves holding down demanding jobs in addition to doing almost everything they had always done at home—taking the primary care and responsibility for children and household. Working women who were married and had families were compelled by circumstances to be superwomen—perfect at everything that was demanded of them. It was not unusual for a woman to remark that her husband "allowed" her to work as long as dinner was on the table when he came home.

"My mother was one of those superwomen," writes Amy. "She ran from six a.m. till midnight."

Women like Amy's mother will recall the joke: "What every executive woman needs is a wife."

The lifestyle of these superwomen became known as "having it all." This meant having the fulfillment of husband, home, children, *and* career. Many scholarly studies at the time purported to show that women were bound to crack under the strain—yet, probably to the surprise of many of those who conducted that research, other studies turned up evidence that there was less depression and generally better life satisfaction among career women than among housewives. It was housewives, not working women, who had the highest rate of entry into psychiatric treatment of any occupational group. And it was housewives who consumed the greatest quantity of mood-modifying drugs. As an article in the *International Journal of Women's Studies* points out, physical and social isolation of housewives, along with their economic dependency within traditional marriage, were considered to be contributing factors.

A pharmaceutical company's ad in a medical journal at that time showed a woman sitting on a folding chair in a school auditorium and looking very depressed. The caption read, "B.A., M.B.A., P.T.A." The ad suggested that the solution for this woman's despondency was a mood-altering drug to cheer her up.

Some studies also claimed that the children of the having-it-all mothers were sure to be emotionally damaged. To this day there is no reliable evidence that the children of employed mothers thrive any less (or more, for that matter) than children of mothers who work only in the home. Other factors seem to be weigh more in determining a child's well-being.

The arguments about whether or not married women, or mothers of young children, should work are academic today. Most women, including those with young children, *are* working, either by economic necessity or by choice. Having it all means less rest and less leisure for women, and in most cases greater stress, but today's economy, combined with the aspirations and independence of today's women, make it unlikely that the workplace and the family alike will ever again be as they were a few decades ago. Women will not give up their hard-won gains in self-determination or economic independence.

But there's a down side. In recent years, many women are beginning to see that, while there is no way they will abandon their careers, combining a life on the fast track with raising a family is not as easy as it sounds. Few of these women can count on equally shared responsibilities from husbands. And American society has not changed to accommodate the needs of working women and their children.

The United States spends less per capita on its children than any other industrialized society in the world. Day care is inadequate and often poor. Few corporations provide it; communities almost reluctantly set it up only for a small percentage of the most needy. Maternity leave, much less paternity leave, is far from available or adequate for most families. Corporations that allow job sharing and flexible time are rare.

Many married career women agonize over the time they lose when they leave their jobs to raise a family. In the near past, it was not only accepted but taken for granted that women who could afford it would leave their jobs when they started their families, perhaps never to return to full-time employment. Today women must worry about time lost from their careers and the likely difficulties of re-entry. These problems are totally foreign to the experience of men. It has always been unthinkable for men to have to choose between career and family.

The average age of first marriage for women has risen in the last 30 years. One sociological study in 1980 found that while most women still in their early 20's who intend to continue working indefinitely do plan to marry and combine their careers with raising a family, there is evidence that as women grow older, they realize how difficult it would be.

These concerns are not lost on the women surveyed for this book. While virtually all indicated that they planned to continue in their careers at least for the foreseeable future, some of those who do hope to marry and have children are aware of the sacrifices they would undoubtedly have to make.

"I see trying to 'have it all' as wanting pie in the sky," says Mary. "Superwomen look pretty wiped out to me and seem to have very little time to themselves. I did at one time aspire to the modern women image, but I have since decided that having and raising children involves too many constraints. Now that I am 40 years old and have passed the safe child-bearing years, I have rethought what I want out of life."

"The women I know who fit the superwoman image walk on a pretty tight rope and are dealing with a lot of stress," Beth, the veterinarian, observes. "I'd try to avoid it, myself."

"I have great respect for women who try to have it all," comments a 36-year-old. "Society is not supportive of children and working mothers. Businesses don't seem to give a damn about children, even though they will be the consumers of the future. Not until corporations become more supportive of working women and their children would I consider having a child."

"I don't aspire to be a superwoman and reach the top of my profession," says Laura. "I want to stay at a comfortable level. However, I do think combining a family and a career is doable provided you have lots of support from a husband and employed help. Superwoman can't be accomplished without superman."

"I think you can combine a career with a husband and family if you really want to," states Jenny. "For me, now, career is first. A relationship, when I'm ready for it, would be second. I'm looking for one good monogamous relationship. I would not want to raise children on my own, but with shared parenting, I might try it."

Barbara agrees. "I'd try to do it all—to have the perfect relationship, perfect children, house, career. It's a fine ideal, even if we can't fully actualize it."

"I don't see having it all as being easy, or just sweetness and light," says a 30-year-old. "If you can choose to stay home, you can be very frustrated—you miss being in the adult world. But if you continue to practice your profession, you can also feel ambivalent because you want to be at home. Whatever you choose, there are bound to be compromises. You have to balance the scale."

So, is having it all something she aspires to? "Yes," she replies.

Doris

This relatively young mother, the pediatric nurse who spoke of having wanted to go to medical school, is divorced and dating. "I have some of the same problems my daughter Jane has in finding intellectually interesting, desirable men to go out with," she says.

Doris is the mother of two sons as well as a daughter, all unmarried. She blames the unhappy relationship she had with their father for the fact that her children are extremely cautious about becoming involved.

Although she does not pressure her 27-year-old daughter (a statement Jane confirms), she worries sometimes because she thinks Jane would like to have a family. In fact, Doris says, "I would encourage her to have children, with or without a husband, because it is a gratifying experience all women should try. I believe having children, nursing and raising them, makes a woman more whole. I loved having my children and would feel incomplete if I hadn't had any."

Doris thinks the expectations of young men and women about marriage have changed greatly. "In my day, women went to college as a backup in case something happened that made their husbands unable to support them. Women were not expected to work after marriage and children. I was an exception—I worked throughout marriage, as in fact my own mother did," she relates. "Today, women are encouraged to get an education with a view to supporting themselves whether they have a family or not."

Asked if she thinks being a superwoman and having it all is realistic, Doris said it's hard, but not impossible. "I did it myself, at a time when support for this role was not great. However, I was in a 9 to 5 job, which allowed me to be home at a reasonable hour. My husband encouraged me to work, but also wanted me to do everything at home," she recalls. "Young men today are more willing to share some of the household responsibilities. With the right career and the right man, it's realistic to try to be a superwoman."

Love and Companionship

Both the professional literature and several recent popular books have reported case after case of career women experiencing role strain or role-conflict when their dedication to their jobs clashes with demands made on them as traditional wives. In her job, a working wife is competing with non-married careerists, both men and women, and with married men who often as not have helpmate wives. At home, having it all usually means doing it all; even if she has household help, she is nevertheless in charge of planning meals, getting house and laundry cleaned, seeing that children are supervised and cared for, keeping their dental appointments and the like, and attending to routine details.

Virtually none of the daughters surveyed for this book see financial security as an important reason for marrying, obviously because they feel they can provide that for themselves. They voted for love and companionship as the primary reasons. They added others: emotional support, intimacy, respect, commitment, a desire to share life's experiences, "best-friendship."

If these qualities are what they are seeking in marriage, they may have difficulty finding partners. Most men in our culture are not conditioned to give emotional support and to regard marriage as a partnership in which the benefits and responsibilities are shared equally. As they see it, if they provide financial and material security for their wives and families, isn't that enough? The psychologist Jesse Bernard states that while the 'good provider' role has been devalued, no concomitant role men are capable of filling has replaced it.

"Marriage should be a cooperative relationship rather than a dependent state for a woman," says a St. Louis woman.

"I would want a relationship in which the man would contribute 50 percent to every aspect of our life together," states another.

"I have never viewed marriage as a goal or a haven," says a 30-year-old Philadelphia woman. "A lot of marriages I see aren't happy. Unless I marry for what I consider the right reasons—love and companionship—instead of financial advantage or a response to pressure, I would rather be alone."

Many sociologists speculate that women's expectations of equality in marriage have advanced faster than men's. Andrew Cherlin suggests that one reason for declining marriage rates may be that "some men, unable to adjust to the changing situation of women, are less actively seeking marriage partners."

There may also be a lack of agreement between men and women as to what constitutes an equitable division of labor within the home. The ironic observation that some men believe taking out the garbage means doing an equal share is only half a joke. When surveys have been made of "liberated" couples, in which the husband, and sometimes even the wife too, believe their marriage is egalitarian, an actual computing of time spent by each on household tasks shows that the notion of shared responsibility is a myth.

Some of the daughters who participated in the survey for this book were asked in telephone interviews if they believe men and women want the same things from marriage. They were mixed in their opinions.

"No," said one. "Both want security, but different kinds. Men want a stable home base in order to pursue their careers. Women want emotional support, and in my opinion they usually don't get it."

"I believe both men and women are looking for emotional support and security," stated Mary, who lives with her lover. "But I am beginning to realize that I must fulfill many of my own needs; I don't expect a man to do it all. It took me a long time to meet a man who fulfills me emotionally, intellectually, and physically, which is a lot. Men like him are rare."

The Dual-Career Couple

Both the mothers' and daughters' surveys described a hypothetical two-career couple in which a decision had to be made regarding the wife's career. In the scenario, the wife had been offered a job in a city 100 miles away that offered a substantial raise in salary and prestige. The question was posed: How would you feel about her accepting the position 1) if it meant the couple had to live apart a few days a week, or 2) if the husband found a new job in the other city but at a somewhat lower salary, or 3) if the wife wanted to take the job but the husband didn't like it. (See **Appendices A and B**.)

The fictional dilemma is meaningful. Traditionally, if the situation were reversed, and the husband was offered the better job, the question of the wife's quitting her own job to move with him wouldn't even come up. Today, however, cases such as the one described and the questions they provoke arise more frequently.

The mothers did not uniformly object to the wife's accepting the job offer. Many thought that if both partners were amenable, then she should take it. But others worried that if the husband had to take a pay cut, his ego would be irreparably damaged. They also felt that the separation would strain the marriage, perhaps even provide the opportunity for adultery. Some saw the career sacrifice on the part of the wife as a natural part of marriage.

Not June, the teacher. While she felt that the couple should not live apart if there were children, she was not especially sympathetic to the husband's objections. And if he had to take a salary cut—"Fine!" June said. "Women have been making this type of compromise for years."

The daughters saw the issue as negotiable. "The couple should discuss it thoroughly and weigh all the advantages and drawbacks," was their general refrain. Fewer than 10 percent of them flatly rejected any of the possibilities described in the scenario. Both mothers and daughters objected least to the couple living apart during the week, and saw the most trouble ahead when the husband was unhappy with the idea.

Approximately one-fifth of mothers and daughters thought the wife should go ahead and take the job over the husband's objections. However, some, like June, pointed out that women have traditionally been forced to pull up stakes and move with their husbands, often without being consulted and perhaps with great reluctance.

One 29-year-old attorney thought the scenario did not indicate all the factors that needed to be considered. "Are there children?" she asked. "Are they in school? Has the husband moved before for the wife's career development? Has she moved for his?" Good questions.

Generally, the daughters' answers to this part of the survey are in keeping with their view of marriage. Their idea of equality and partnership in marriage apparently leads them to view the wife's career as of equal importance to the husband's. Where jobs are concerned, they see automatic acquiescence to the husband's preferences to be unacceptable.

Virginia

This mother, though somewhat older than most of the mothers surveyed, is active in a range of community work, has wide interests, and holds quite contemporary views. She feels success at a career is just as important for a woman as it is for a man, and that the hypothetical two-career couple described in the survey should negotiate the dilemma so the wife could accept the promotion.

Virginia, who worked after high school and then went on to college and graduate school, had a career as an editor on a local newspaper, though part-time during the years when her children were growing up. "My own mother was widowed and went to work," she says. "I was a latch-key child in 1918—imagine it!"

Virginia is sympathetic to women today in their efforts and their frequent sacrifices to fulfill their desires for both a career and family. She understands the risks they may be taking if they drop out to have children. And she believes that men have not completely come around to doing their share at home.

Asked if she would be supportive if her 33-year-old unmarried daughter chose to have a child without being married, she had this to say: "I'm glad that I had the opportunity to be married and that there were two of us to raise our family. But increasing numbers of young women today realize that they will never have the love and joy of raising children unless they do it themselves as single parents. If my daughter wanted to have a child, I would be confident that she had considered all angles, the hardships as well as the happiness, and then, if she decided to go ahead, I would really support her in it."

Virginia does not worry whether her daughter will marry or not. "I think she probably hoped to get married when she was younger, but now I think she is accepting of the fact that she may not. She feels good about herself as a person and is far from desperate. I don't believe she is actively searching for a man. She has an interesting life as it is," says Virginia.

7

Support

''Her decision-making
skills are
superb''

One of the burdens of being human is our vulnerability to loneliness. It is the penalty for our capacity for love and our desire for friendship. We need to bond. Loneliness is not confined to human beings—many other social animals, including apes, dolphins, elephants, and hundreds of other species, suffer and can die from lack of contact with their own kind.

In the survey for this book, the major reason mothers gave for worrying about their unmarried daughters was that they didn't want them to be lonely. Three-quarters of the mothers indicated that a good reason for a man or woman to marry was for companionship, especially in old age. The image of the traditional "old maid" in literature, cartoon, film, and folklore is of a lonely and loveless spinster.

The confirmed bachelor—the old maid's counterpart—is not wrapped in the same negative imagery. He is variously viewed as bon vivant or hermit, clever or eccentric, but usually as a person alone by choice rather than by rejection. (Ironically, he has even been given the sobriquet "lone wolf," a misnomer indeed. That much maligned animal in fact lives in a highly social group and is devoted to family, monogamous for life.)

The daughters who answered the questionnaire, some of whom *do* worry about being viewed as "old maids," do not seem to lack companionship. Of those who aren't living with lovers or involved in exclusive relationships, most indicated that they would like to be dating, whether or not their dates led to permanent relationships. But does this mean they are lonely, leading impoverished personal lives?

Friendship

Friendships are important elements in the lives of the women surveyed for this book. They appear to have an abundance of friends whom they value: All reported at least one close female friend and almost half mentioned three or four good women friends. For some, all their close friends are women. Additionally, they don't confine their social circle to other single people—three-quarters of them have women friends who are married.

"I don't think you can have a true, complete friendship with a man," says Andrea. "I have a boyfriend whom I hope to marry, and male colleagues whom I like very much, and I once had a real buddy who was gay. But my closest friends are women.

"Men experience life entirely differently from women. It's just not possible for them to understand things the way another woman can."

Despite Andrea's reservations, nearly half of the women surveyed indicate that they count one or two men among their closest friends.

"Men are a great source of friendship for me," says Jenny. "My most satisfying relationships are with men who have been my lovers and best friends, and then remained friends afterward."

One woman indicated she had eight close friends, men and women—she apparently felt she couldn't leave any one of them out. "I know, eight is more than the five asked for on the questionnaire," she wrote, "but these eight have proved tried and true."

As discussed in Chapter 4, over 80 percent of the women indicated that they believe friends and an active social life are just as crucial for happiness as a spouse. Half said they have less time to spend with friends than they would like. Even the majority of those who are living with lovers or involved in exclusive relationships claimed they don't see their friends enough. The fact that these women often find it hard to divide their free time between lovers and friends suggests that close friends may be of almost equal importance to them.

Among their friends, there is little competitiveness. Asked if they think their friends resent their career success, only two women felt this was a problem with any real frequency. One-half felt their friends are never or rarely jealous of them.

Less than half of the women report spending more than 30

percent of their free time alone, whether they are dating or not. Women who are not dating spend about 20 percent of their free time on hobbies, which is slightly more than women who are dating.

Close involvement with a lover, and even dating, creates a difference in how time is apportioned with large groups of friends. Women who are dating tend to spend little of their free time with groups of friends, and choose instead to share that time with one or two close friends. Conversely, women who are not currently dating report spending quite a lot of their free time not only with close friends but also with groups with whom they share common interests. They might belong to a bridge club, or socialize with a hobby group, a foreign language class, or colleagues from work. The many interests of these women put them in frequent contact with like-minded people. Women not dating are also, not surprisingly, likely to spend more time with their families.

Several women not currently involved with lovers spontaneously commented on their questionnaires of feeling sufficiently sustained and happy in their other personal relationships. "I like my independence and get plenty of support and pleasure from my friends and family," said Emily.

Linda, remember, mentioned that close friends can create a family for single people.

Gail quoted a friend of hers as saying, "We need our friends to get us through our relationships!"

In follow-up telephone interviews, a small sample of women were asked to expand on the importance of friends and family: "In the event that you do not marry, do you think you will have the emotional support and fulfillment you will need? Can you describe where or from whom you expect this support will come?"

Virtually all the women responded positively and had a lot to say on the subject of friends and family. It didn't seem to make much difference whether they were also currently involved with lovers or not.

"I learned long ago to count on my friends for support," said a Portland woman.

"I'll get all the support I need from my family," replied Amy. "I think I have that now. We don't have problems communicating our feelings to each other, or giving hugs and kisses and pats on the back. In my family I have never felt unloved."

"I am presently living with a man who is supportive," said Mary. "But since I don't intend to marry, I expect I'll receive enough emotional support and fulfillment from my friends and family. I have an especially close friend in my sister."

"Right now I am in a primary relationship, but if I weren't, I would count on support from my friends," said another. "I know if I need them they'll be there."

One woman who has married since completing the survey said she still derives much support from her friends and family. "Being married hasn't changed that," she said. "My male and female friends visit us at home two or three times a week. I pride myself on maintaining these friendships."

Barbara said she gets most of her support from family and friends now. "The support in a friendship is a lot deeper and longer lasting than what you get in a romantic relationship," she added. "I think friends can fill emotional needs better than a significant other, at least over the long term."

Jenny makes a distinction between the support of a relationship and that of friendship. "In friendships, you don't have a lot of expectations. In relationships, expectations can get in the way."

Kate spoke of a close extended family and a network of women friends. "And I belong to a church, clubs, and several groups that provide me with support and fulfillment."

Gloria also mentioned feeling fulfilled from her contacts in the civic and community groups she belongs to—"I have developed many friendships among people with whom I share common interests," she said. "Also, I have a sister and a circle of close female friends, and we support each other."

As mentioned earlier, over one-third of the women surveyed for this book have dogs or cats, or both. In recent years, there has been a great deal of interest in the relationships between people and their companion animals. Scholarly and scientific studies indicate that pets are far more important in our lives than former mainstream opinion has suggested, and the new findings have outdated the notion that affectional relationships between fellow humans are the only legitimate ones. Some research has focused on the role of pets in the lives of people who live alone, and for many they help to fill a need for love and companionship, for play and humor.

In subsequent telephone interviews, several of these women were asked about their feelings for their pets.

"I couldn't live without a pet," said one woman. "My dog and two cats give companionship, and I like being responsible for these lives that I derive so much pleasure from. Also, they serve as a channel of communication between me and my brother—he always wants to know how they're doing, and we talk a lot about them."

"I thought having a pet would be a burden, but that hasn't been the case," said Kate. "I like having another creature in the house with me."

"My dog and two cats give stability and responsibility to my life," said another.

One woman listed "playing with my dog" as one of her leisure-time activities.

Though some women have dogs (one reported having three), most have chosen cats, possibly because working women living alone might find cats somewhat easier to care for than dogs.

"My cats are a source of great comfort to me," said Amy. "They're nice to come home to. I never feel alone."

Laura spoke affectionately about her two cats, which she has had for seven years. "I receive a lot from them, both emotionally and physically," she stated.

Lynn said her two cats are her best friends. "I love to come home and hug my cats," she added. "They are a big part of my good mental health."

"My cats were especially important to me during the 10 years I lived alone," said Mary. "It was nice to come home to those warm, cuddly bodies."

Even the woman who has recently married feels her cats are very important to her emotionally. "They not only provide me with physical comfort, but my black cat, who has been with me for 12 years—I think of him as my alter-ego," she stated.

Only one woman reported dumping her pet when it became inconvenient to keep him. "I was just enchanted by him at first, but as I got busier, he became less important to me," she said.

Marcia

"Marriage is a nice public symbol for anyone who wants it," says this 30-year-old clinical psychologist who lives in

Portland. Marcia lives with her lover and says marriage is not an option. At 18, she did not assume she would be married by her current age. Her parents were divorced when she was a teenager, but Marcia doesn't believe that turned her off—"I had other types of relationships to look at, including good marriages."

Marcia says her mother does not pressure her to marry, and her mother indicated that she does not worry about her daughter—"She is happy single." Mother and daughter speak to each other several times a week: "I call her or she calls me. It's about even." She says that when she was growing up, her mother gave her the sense that she could do anything she wanted, and had high expectations of her. She thinks this encouraged her to aim high.

Marcia thinks having it all is realistic if you have a supportive husband and a relatively stable career situation. "If you marry someone who expects you to come home and do everything after working all day, you'll kill yourself," she says. "Or, if you had a young child at home, it would be very difficult to go through a major job change at the same time. I often find it hard to manage time for friends and family, and to make it to all family events. Sometimes no one is happy. But I think if you have someone to really share responsibilities with you, it can be done. Having it all is a balancing act."

Asked if she believes men and women want the same things from marriage, she says, "Both men and women want companionship, but I personally don't think you can get everything from one person. We are socialized to believe, romantically, that one person will fulfill all our needs, but in fact we need other people as well."

Marcia's mother, asked how she feels about the man Marcia is living with, is concise: "Fine!"

Options

"I no longer see marriage as the solution to loneliness or insecurity," says Dianne, who at 37 is the manager of a large retail store. "I see friends in unhappy marriages, I see that 50 percent of all marriages in this country end in divorce, and I realize that my situation as an independent, single woman is healthier than many marriages. Also, I find great fulfillment in my social contact with friends and family, and in my career.

"I might like to be married some day, but I am cautious. And I won't feel I'm a failure if I don't marry. I can provide financial security for myself, and I get plenty of emotional fulfillment elsewhere."

Linda feels more or less as Dianne does. "I do interesting work, make a decent salary, contribute to the community, and spend my time well," she states. "All in all, I'm generally happy with my life."

A lesbian woman comments: "I don't really want to be married. I am interested in women as well as men, but not in any one relationship full time."

Another lesbian woman believes that many heterosexual marriages take place because the couple feels it's expected of them. "If I were to marry, it would be to a woman, as a celebration and outward declaration of commitment to a partnership for life," she says.

"I no longer consider marriage necessary for my happiness or well-being, or even for motherhood if I should want it," states a 34-year-old successful New York executive.

Another says: "I don't feel that a woman has to be married to be fulfilled. Marriage is not the only option available to a woman in order for her to be considered a success in adult life."

Lynn sums up: "Over the years I've come to realize that there are options. At first, I felt there must be something wrong with me. Then it dawned on me that not being married was just fine with me, and that's what was important. It took some time, but it happened."

A number of women have spoken of fulfilling their desire for children, in the event that they do not marry, by adopting or by deliberately becoming pregnant and going it alone. Eight mothers selected from the survey were asked, in telephone interviews, if they felt they could be supportive of their daughters if they had children "out of wedlock."

The mothers did not believe that it would be easy for their daughters to raise children alone, but all but two stated that they would be supportive. "I hope that my daughter would not undertake having and raising a child alone—she would certainly have to be very financially secure, for one thing. But if she did have a child, I would certainly be supportive of her," said Sylvia. And Doris, remember, said she would encourage her daughter to have a child, with or without a husband, so she wouldn't miss the experience.

This matter may be increasingly relevant, as rising numbers of unmarried women are deciding to go ahead and bear children before age makes pregnancy risky or impossible. While unwed teenagers are commonly thought to account for every rise in non-marital births, the National Center for Health Statistics reported in 1986 a rise in non-marital birth rates in every age group *except* among women aged 15 to 17. The Center study accounts for the higher rate among single women in their 30's and 40's by several factors: the widespread tendency among women to delay marriage to increasingly older ages, the high divorce rate, and the gradual rise in social acceptability of motherhood outside of marriage.

In view of what many single women today call the shortage of "good" men, those who strongly wish to have children, whose biological clocks are sounding alarms, and who can adequately support children themselves may not be willing to wait for suitable husbands to come along.

June

A highly educated professional, this East Coast mother pursues her own career—teaching—and is a recognized expert in learning-disabled children. She has been married 35 years and is the mother of four grown children, grandmother of three.

June married at 20 but believes that age is much too young today. "Young people now should live independently before marrying, should support themselves and explore the world a bit before settling down," she says.

She worries sometimes about her accomplished 38-year-old unmarried daughter because she doesn't want her to be lonely, but according to her daughter, she does not pressure. Asked if she thinks her daughter should be doing more to find a partner, June says, "Only if she wants to be married."

She and her daughter see eye-to-eye on the qualities that they would consider undesirable in a son-in-law/

spouse, except that June is more particular—she thinks her daughter should have a husband who is physically attractive and as intelligent as she, qualities that don't especially matter to her daughter.

"I worry less now about her getting married than I did when she was 25 or 26," June continues. " She is busy and active and seems content. I no longer think she will get married, and if it doesn't bother her, then it doesn't bother me."

Asked if she thinks it is realistic for today's women to try to combine career with husband and children, June believes it can be done but the woman gives up a lot. "I had the best of both worlds," she recalls. "I didn't work until my children were in school."

If her daughter had a child without being married, June expressed strong reservations about the hardships and sacrifices single parenthood places on women. "But of course I would be supportive of her," she says.

The Women: A Summary

The women who have emerged in composite portraits from the survey and interviews for this book are quite different from the woefully resigned or frantically desperate unmarried women so often portrayed in the popular media.

In a nutshell, many of the women would like to marry, but they refuse to settle or compromise just for the sake of being wives. Some of the women definitely prefer to remain single; some are unsure. Well over half have either turned down explicit proposals or have deflected possible proposals by making it clear that those relationships were not going to lead to marriage.

"I've enjoyed some very supportive relationships that I knew would not have turned into good marriages," said a 28-year-old Washington, D.C. woman. "By expressing this nonverbally, the relationships could find their own place without anyone having to suffer an outright rejection."

If the women were to marry, it would be for love and companionship, and they would seek truly equal partnerships. "At 18, I would have expected to be dependent on my spouse," said a woman in her 30's. "Now, I would expect to be fully equal."

Whether or not they are aware of the disparity in the ratio of available single men to single women because of the "baby boom," many of the women speak of a shortage of "good" men. By good, they mean men who, in addition to having other desirable qualities, would be equal partners in a marriage rather than men who would expect the traditional type of marriage most of them were raised in.

The women consider emotional support as a more important reason to marry than financial security, which they feel is either transitory, given today's divorce rate, or something they can provide for themselves.

They feel they are pressured to marry by society in general and by their family members and friends. Their mothers, who may or may not be a source of pressure, worry about them, especially for fear that they might be lonely. (One woman claims her *sister* pressures her to marry for a similar reason: "It's not that she doesn't want me to be lonely, she just wants me to be lonely *with* somebody, like she is—she's married!")

If not dating, the women would like to be. Many indicated that they would prefer to be dating much more than they are, and mentioned finding it difficult to meet suitable men.

But are they necessarily lonely, leading socially impoverished lives? This does not seem to be the case. Over 70 percent of those surveyed indicated that one reason fewer professional women were marrying was because they enjoy the independence that living alone affords them. The fact that this was the most common response suggests that in their view, singlehood has a lot going for it.

All are very or at least fairly successful in their careers and hope to advance. Career commitment appears strong among most of the women. Nearly half are in managerial or professional work; some plan to make career changes, get further education, or go into business for themselves. Almost all expect to be working for the next 15 years, though a few indicated that if they married and had children, they would stop temporarily. Asked what they would do if they suddenly came into a large amount of money, some said they would switch to work that they enjoyed more, but only three said they would quit working altogether.

They appear ambitious—on a self-placement scale in terms of their goals, most saw their current positions as somewhere in the middle, suggesting that they plan to move ahead.

On the matter of having it all, that is, combining career with husband and children—becoming superwomen—the women's responses were mixed. Some said they would try to do it, others saw it as a route to burnout. While many thought it was possible with a supportive partner who shared work and responsibilities, they are aware of the hardships as things now stand in the 1980s in the United States, with the scarcity of quality day care, flexible time, and other supports for working mothers. Most of their own mothers also expressed concern about the high price of being a superwoman.

The qualms women have about the costs of having it all do not mean that they have decided to chuck the hard-won advances or pass up the opportunities and return to the scene of their mother's era. The women are saying they want true choices. Those women who choose to continue their careers while running a home and raising children must have some help from society, including from corporate America, the kind of accommodations already in place in many other countries.

Rhoda, the mother who is a social worker, says that in her experience, women who had both jobs and children were more purposeful and respected themselves more than the mothers who worked only at home. She thinks women can have both careers and families—especially if we upgrade our day care services, "like Sweden, for example," she says.

In addition to career gratification, and the contacts and activities related to their work, the women seem to have an abundance of friendships that fill their lives. They receive support and fulfillment from their friends. Even those living with lovers indicate that they still depend to a large extent on friends to fill these needs.

As we have seen, all reported at least one close female friend; many mentioned three or four. Many enjoy the friendship of men; over a third of the women claimed at least two good male friends. They report that they spend less time with their friends than they would like; even those who are living with or involved in exclusive dating relationships with lovers felt that they didn't see their friends enough, suggesting that friendships are central to the lives of these women. And as noted, the women do not seem to feel any resentment from their friends concerning their successes in their careers.

Women with lovers or significant others continue to spend time with one or two close friends—in fact, they spend nearly as much time this way as do women who have no lovers or dates in their lives. Apparently, being involved with a lover or dates doesn't mean they drop their close friends. A difference did show up in the time spent with groups of friends: Women who are not dating spend perhaps twice as much time with groups of friends as do women who have lovers or dates.

All the women in the survey seem to recognize that they need some time to relax alone. They spend 15 to 30 percent of their free time alone relaxing or pursuing hobbies, but considering the demanding types of work many of them are engaged in, time for themselves would seem essential. Women who are not dating spend somewhat more time on hobbies or activities that they can enjoy alone. But women who are dating and those who are not spend about the same amount of time in some form of solitary relaxation.

At the end of the survey, the women were asked what activities and hobbies they pursue in their leisure time. What a wide range of interests showed up. The women go to concerts, films, museums, and ballet. They take courses—ceramics, dance, exercise. They run, bike, swim, play tennis, hike, ski. They read, watch TV, listen to music, travel. Some do volunteer work in community or charitable organizations. They sew, garden, entertain their friends. These women are certainly not sitting home waiting for the phone to ring.

This summary of single professional women should help to answer the question many mothers ask: "Why isn't my daughter married?"

Mothers and Daughters

On the subject of unmarried women and their mothers, popular wisdom has it that the relationship is often antagonistic: nagging mothers and resentful daughters. While some of that was revealed in the survey, on the whole this supposition was not totally borne out.

The mothers agree their daughters should be selective, and judging from the qualities they would not want in sons-in-law, they believe their daughters deserve the best.

While many mothers do worry about their unmarried daughters, others do not, and both worriers and non-worriers are very often supportive. A large proportion of the daughters feel tremendous social pressure to marry, but not necessarily from their mothers.

Many of the mother/daughter relationships came across as warm and understanding.

Some of the women were asked if they thought any of their success in their lives was attributable to their mothers. Most did.

"My mother always encouraged me to be independent, self-reliant, and to pursue an education," said Gloria. "She was an excellent role model."

"Both my parents were always supportive and told me I could become anything I wanted," Mary stated, "but my mother, who never went to college and was so encouraging when I did, was definitely the stronger influence."

Kate referred to the fact that her mother had her own profession, which she enjoyed, but also, "There are a lot of single women in my family who have been good role models for me."

Another daughter similarly mentioned that her mother had held a job and liked it. "She gained recognition and respect," said this woman. "I think it made her a better mother."

"She was always willing to support me and listen to my concerns and the details of my activities," Amy said of her mother, who is deceased. "Sharing was easy and reciprocal. She was my best friend." (What mother would not want to have such a tribute from her daughter?)

In general, the mothers, whether or not they were worried about their daughters' chances of marrying, often spoke positively about their daughters' lives and supported them either verbally and directly or by not interfering.

"She is her own person and dislikes suggestions," said a mother whose daughter reports no pressure.

Another non-pressuring mother states, "I believe my daughter would rather be married but is not terribly unhappy being single. She would rather be single than in an unhappy marriage." Asked if she thought her daughter should be doing more to find a suitable partner, this mother said, "Possibly, but she already has an active social life."

And as one mother views her daughter's situation: "She keeps very busy in many interesting activities where men are included and doesn't sit around feeling sorry for herself. I believe she will make her life rewarding, whatever comes."

It might be suggested that if the media would stop describing the lives of unmarried women with such condescending pity and patronizing assumptions of forlorn solitude, this mother's daughter, and women like her, will stand a better chance of continuing to enjoy the rewarding single life she apparently has already created for herself.

It is no accident that there is only one admirable never-married female character in a major television show—gorgeous, ambitious, and independent Christine Cagney, who has been aptly described as flamboyantly single. But predatory comic singles and divorced dingbats abound.

The letters in response to the *New York Times* article, "Coping with the Void," mentioned in Chapter 1, included one from an annoyed woman who wrote sarcastically, "Thanks for running that neat article on how single women feel sorry for themselves. It wasn't the least bit slanted. I look forward to the rest of the series . . . 'Single Men: Living Alone and Loving It (Desperate Women Available by the Score).' " An epidemiologist was appalled at the article's research: "There was no attempt to draw a representative and balanced cross-section of single women." And a Ph.D. candidate in women's history asked, "Why does society compel women to choose between a career and marriage, while for men that is a natural combination? Both the content and tone of the article suggest that many women are not making the right choices. The career woman who has chosen much the same path toward self-fulfillment that men have traditionally taken finds herself at a moment when male-female socialization patterns have not caught up with reality."

It would greatly help single women withstand pressure from society if more mothers understood that not all of them necessarily wish to marry, that those who would like to marry are nevertheless not willing to settle for less than totally egalitarian marriages, that unmarried women can and do have happy and fulfilled lives, that daughters today are committed to their careers, and that daughters feel supported and enriched by their friendships. Perhaps then whatever tension that exists between them and their unmarried daughters could be dispelled.

"It would be nice if everyone accepted the fact that some of us are happy with our lifestyles and don't want to change," comments Barbara.

"When I'm pressured by my relatives and married friends, it makes me feel lonely and sad that I don't have a husband," says a 27-year-old real estate broker. "But then I remind myself that I don't have to be married to be happy. In fact, I think I have a fine life on my own—the problem is explaining this to them!"

Daughter's Survey

Name ____
Address ____
____
____
Phone # ____
____

1. For each of the following statements, please tell us to what extent you agree or disagree.

   a) In order to feel happy and fulfilled in her life, a woman must be married.
   ___ agree strongly ___somewhat agree ___not sure
   ___disagree somewhat ___disagree strongly

   b) Success at a career is not as important for a woman as it is for a man.
   ___agree strongly ___somewhat agree ___not sure
   ___disagree somewhat ___disagree strongly

   c) Friends and an active social life are just as crucial to a woman's happiness and well-being as a spouse.
   ___agree strongly ___somewhat agree ___not sure
   ___disagree somewhat ___disagree strongly

   d) A woman with young children should not work outside the home.
   ___agree strongly ___somewhat agree ___not sure
   ___disagree somewhat ___disagree strongly

   e) Women should not have children outside of marriage.
   ___agree strongly ___somewhat agree ___not sure
   ___disagree somewhat ___disagree strongly

   f) A woman should take her husband's name when she marries.
   ___agree strongly ___somewhat agree ___not sure
   ___disagree somewhat ___disagree strongly

   g) Young women today are more selfish than other generations were.

___agree strongly ___somewhat agree ___not sure
___disagree somewhat ___disagree strongly

2. What do you consider the best reasons for a woman to marry? (check all that apply)
   ___ economic security
   ___ love
   ___ raise children
   ___ legitimize sexual relations
   ___ companionship, especially in old age
   ___ other (specify) ______________________________

3. What do you consider the best reasons for a man to marry? (check all that apply)
   ___ economic security
   ___ love
   ___ raise children
   ___ legitimize sexual relations
   ___ companionship, especially in old age
   ___ other (specify) ______________________________

4. Why do you think fewer young professional women are marrying these days? (check as many reasons as you think appropriate)
   ___ too high standards for prospective husband
   ___ their high status intimidates men
   ___ shortage of men
   ___ they enjoy the independence living on their own affords
   ___ careers don't allow time for much personal life
   ___ they are too old
   ___ men are too demanding in what they expect women to give up for marriage
   ___ other (specify) ______________________________

5. Think for a moment about a family where both the husband and wife work at good jobs they enjoy. The wife is offered a substantial promotion in both salary and prestige. The job is in a city 100 miles away. How do you feel about her accepting the new job if:
   a) it means the couple has to live apart a few days a week? ________
   ____
   ____

   b) the husband finds a job similar to his present one at a somewhat lower salary? ______________________________
   ____
   ____

c) the wife wants to take the job but her husband doesn't particularly like it? ______________________________

____

____

6. What is your occupation? ______________________________

7. How long have you worked at your present job? ______________

8. Think for a moment about your career goals. In terms of your plans and aspirations, please mark the spot on the scale where you see yourself now. (1 is the lowest mark and 7 is the highest.)

   (low) 1 2 3 4 5 6 7 (high)

9. If you were to come into a large sum of money right now would you
   ___ continue to work at your present job?
   ___ continue to work but at something you enjoyed more, even if it meant volunteering or taking a substantial pay cut?
   ___ quit your job?

10. Do you expect to be working continuously for the next fifteen years?
    ___ yes ___ no ___ not sure
    If yes, do you expect to be at the same job? ______________
    If no, what do you expect to be doing? ______________

11. If you were to marry, would you expect to continue to work at a job outside the home?
    ___ yes ___ no ___ depends

12. Do you find there is a trade-off between the amount of time you devote to your job or advancing your career and that spent with a lover or the people you date?
    ___ yes ___ no ___ not sure

13. Do you ever feel that you place your career aspirations ahead of romantic involvements?
    ___ yes ___ seldom ___ occasionally ___ frequently

14. Have you ever felt that someone you were (are) involved with was (is) uncomfortable with your success at a career?
    ___ yes ___ no ___ not sure
    If yes, how was (is) this manifest? ______________

    ____

15. Do you ever feel that your friends are envious of your career opportunities?
___ never ___ seldom ___ occasionally ___ frequently

16. If you were very excited because you had just received especially high compliments on a project at work or were told about a promotion, who would be the first person you would want to call with the news?
___ best friend
___ mother
___ professional colleague
___ lover
___ other (please specify) ______________________________

17. If you called your mother with this news, can you describe what her reaction would probably be?
____
____
____
____
____
____

18. Do you ever feel that your mother is envious of your career opportunities?
___ never ___ seldom ___ occasionally ___ frequently

19. Is your mother supportive of your career plans and aspirations?
___ always ___ usually ___ seldom

20. Here is a list of qualities which parents sometimes encourage their children to develop. Please check the four which you think were most stressed for you as you were growing up.
___ ambitious
___ popular
___ athletic
___ intelligent
___ creative
___ assertive
___ pretty
___ independent

21. Think for a moment about your five closest friends. Please put a check mark beside the category that describes each of them. (Use more than one check mark on any category if necessary.)

___ single woman ___ single man
___ married woman ___ married man
___ divorced woman ___ divorced man
___ other

22. Do you find there is a trade-off between the amount of time you spend with friends and that spent devoted to your job or advancing your career?
___ yes ___ no ___ not sure

23. Do you find there is a trade-off between the amount of time you spend with friends and that spent with a lover or the people you date?
___ yes ___ no ___ not sure

24. Right now, would you describe the amount of time spent with friends as:
___ more than you would like
___ just about right
___ less than you would like

25. Do you ever feel that someone you date or a lover resents the amount of time you spend with friends and family?
___ never ___ seldom ___ occasionally ___ frequently

26. Do you ever feel that your friends resent the amount of time you spend with a lover or someone you are dating?
___ never ___ seldom ___ occasionally ___ frequently

27. In general, would you say that your free time which is spent in the company of others is:
___ mostly spent with people (or the person) with whom you are romantically attached
___ about half with a romantic involvement and half with friends or family
___ mostly with friends or family

28. Please estimate the percent of your free time you spend in the following ways:
___ alone, relaxing
___ along, pursuing hobbies or activities
___ with family
___ with one or two close friends
___ socializing with a group
___ with a lover or date
___ volunteer work

___ other (please specify) ______________________________

29. Are you currently dating anyone?
    ___ yes, we live together (please answer questions in BOX I)
    ___ yes, I date one person exclusively (skip to BOX II)
    ___ yes, I date a number of people (skip to BOX III)
    ___ no (skip to BOX IV)

BOX I

How long have you been living together? ____________________
How long did you date before moving in together? ____________
Do you expect this relationship to lead to marriage?
___ yes ___ possibly ___ no
If you do not expect your current relationship to lead to marriage, which of the following statements best describes your reasons for this:
___ I would like to marry but this is the wrong person for me.
___ I would like to marry this person but he is unwilling or unable to do so.
___ I enjoy being single and prefer to remain so.
___ Other (please specify) ______________________________
____

BOX II

How long have you been dating? ______________________
Do you expect this relationship to lead to marriage?
___ yes ___ possibly ___ no
If you do not expect your current relationship to lead to marriage, which of the following statements best describes your reasons for this:
___ I would like to marry but this is the wrong person for me.
___ I would like to marry this person but he is unwilling or unable to do so.
___ I enjoy being single and prefer to remain so.
___ Other (please specify) ______________________________
____
____

BOX III

Please list the lengths of all your current relationships:
Do you expect any of these relationships to lead to marriage?

___ yes ___ possibly ___ no

How would you describe your attitude toward dating more than one person?

___ No one person can offer me all that I value in a relationship so I prefer to see a variety of people.
___ At some point I would like to date only one person, but right now I don't feel like making an exclusive commitment.
___ I would prefer to see one person exclusively but none of those I am currently dating meet my standards.
___ Other (please specify) ______________________________
____

BOX IV

How would you characterize your reasons for not dating?

___ I would like to be dating but have not met the right person.
___ At this point in my life, I feel that I need time by myself.
___ Right now my schedule is so hectic, I can't find the time to date.
___ Other (please specify) ______________________________
____
____

30. Would you say that the amount of dating you currently participate in is:
    ___ more than you would like
    ___ just about right
    ___ somewhat less than you would like
    ___ much less than you would like

31. In general, where or how do you meet people to date? (check all that apply)
    ___ through mutual friends
    ___ at work
    ___ church or synagogue
    ___ personal ads
    ___ adult education classes
    ___ singles organizations
    ___ through family members
    ___ bars or clubs
    ___ other (please specify) ______________________________

32. Would you go out with someone if you did not think there was a good chance of developing a serious relationship with that person?
    ___ yes ___ no ___ not sure

33. Please read this list and check those qualities a man might have that would make it absolutely impossible for you to consider marrying him.
   ___ physically unattractive
   ___ made significantly less money than you
   ___ different religion
   ___ refused to participate in household chores
   ___ had a lower level of education than you
   ___ incapable of fathering children
   ___ insisted that you not work outside the home after marriage
   ___ sexually unfulfilling
   ___ more than 5 years younger than you
   ___ had very different political beliefs
   ___ strongly disliked your friends and family
   ___ less intelligent
   ___ other (please specify) ______________________________

34. Have you ever turned down an explicit proposal of marriage?
   ___ yes ___ no (skip to question 35)
   Do you regret having done so?
   ___ yes ___ no
   Please explain why you do or do not regret having done so.
   ____
   ____

35. Have you ever felt that your behavior has pre-empted a proposal of marriage, that is, have you ever made it clear, without saying so, that you were not interested in getting married?
   ___ yes ___ no (skip to question 36)
   ___ not sure (skip to question 36)
   Do you regret having done so?
   ___ yes ___ no
   Please explain why you do or do not regret having done so.
   ____
   ____

36. When you were 18, did you think you would be married by your current age?
   ___ yes ___ no ___ don't remember

37. Do you think your feelings about marriage have changed since that time?
   ___ yes ___ no ___ not sure
   If yes, how have they changed? ______________________________
   ____

____
____
____
____

If no, please describe your feelings about marriage. __________
____
____
____
____
____

38. Do you ever feel pressure from others to marry?
 ___ yes ___ no (skip to question 39) ___ not sure
 If so, from whom? (check all that apply)
 ___ mother
 ___ father
 ___ other relatives
 ___ single friends
 ___ married friends
 ___ co-workers
 ___ other (please specify) __________________
 In what way or ways is this pressure manifest? __________
____
____
____
____
____
____

 How do you usually react to such pressure? __________
____
____
____
____
____
____

39. If you feel that your mother sometimes pressures you about marriage, do you think she does so for any of the following reasons? (check all that apply)
 ___ She thinks you would feel happier if you were married.
 ___ She would like grandchildren.
 ___ She thinks marriage is a better measure of success for a woman

than a good career is.

___ She wants to be able to tell her friends that her daughter is getting married.

___ She thinks your life should be more stable.

___ She feels you are implicitly rejecting her own position as wife and mother by remaining unmarried.

___ She worries about you providing for yourself economically.

___ She doesn't want you to be lonely.

___ Other (please specify) ______________________________

40. About which of the following subjects do you receive advice from your mother?

___ financial matters

___ career

___ friends

___ love

___ education

___ major purchases

41. Which of the following statements come closest to describing the way you discuss your romantic involvements with your mother?

___ I usually discuss most aspects of my relationships with my mother.

___ I talk about my relationships with my mother but I leave out any negative information such as bad habits of my partner or if we are having problems.

___ I rarely talk to my mother about relationships except to mention them in passing.

42. Do you feel that your mother would like to hear more about your relationships than you tell her?

___ yes ___ no ___ not sure

If yes, what keeps you from telling her more? ______________________________

____

____

____

____

____

____

43. How often do you see your mother? ______________________________

44. How often do you speak with her by telephone? ______________________________

45. What is your present living situation?

___ live alone
___ live with parents
___ live with lover
___ live with roommates
    ___ female roommates ___ number
    ___ male roommates ___ number

46. Do you:
    ___ rent apartment
    ___ own apartment
    ___ rent house
    ___ own home
    ___ other

47. What is your educational background?
    ___ college (degree and institution) ______________________
    ___ M.A. or Professional degree ______________________
    ___ Ph.D. (field) ______________________

48. When growing up, did you live in a city with:
    ___ more than 200,000 inhabitants
    ___ between 50,000-200,000 inhabitants
    ___ between 10,000-50,000 inhabitants
    ___ less than 10,000 inhabitants

49. What is your religion?
    ___ Protestant
    ___ Catholic
    ___ Jewish
    ___ Atheist or Agnostic
    ___ Other

50. Would you say in matters of religion, you are
    ___ very religious
    ___ somewhat religious
    ___ not very religious
    ___ not religious at all

51. How large is your place of employment? ______________________

52. What is your current age? ______________________

53. What is your present income? ______________________

54. What activities and hobbies do you participate in outside of work?

____
____
____

55. Do you have any pets? _____
If yes, how many and what type? ____________________

This completes the survey. Thank you very much for your participation.

Mother's Survey

Name ____

Address ____

____

____

Phone # ____

____

1. For each of the following statements, please tell us to what extent you agree or disagree.

   a) In order to feel happy and fulfilled in her life, a woman must be married.
   ___ agree strongly ___ somewhat agree ___ not sure
   ___ disagree somewhat ___ disagree strongly

   b) Success at a career is not as important for a woman as it is for a man.
   ___ agree strongly ___ somewhat agree ___ not sure
   ___ disagree somewhat ___ disagree strongly

   c) Friends and an active social life are just as crucial to a woman's happiness and well-being as a spouse.
   ___ agree strongly ___ somewhat agree ___ not sure
   ___ disagree somewhat ___ disagree strongly

   d) A woman with young children should not work outside the home.
   ___ agree strongly ___ somewhat agree ___ not sure
   ___ disagree somewhat ___ disagree strongly

   e) Women should not have children outside of marriage.
   ___ agree strongly ___ somewhat agree ___ not sure
   ___ disagree somewhat ___ disagree strongly

   f) A woman should take her husband's name when she marries.
   ___ agree strongly ___ somewhat agree ___ not sure
   ___ disagree somewhat ___ disagree strongly

   g) Young women today are more selfish than other generations were.

___ agree strongly ___ somewhat agree ___ not sure
___ disagree somewhat ___ disagree strongly

2. What do you consider the best reasons for a woman to marry? (check all that apply)
   ___ economic security
   ___ love
   ___ raise children
   ___ legitimize sexual relations
   ___ companionship, especially in old age
   ___ other (specify) ______________________________

3. What do you consider the best reasons for a man to marry? (check all that apply)
   ___ economic security
   ___ love
   ___ raise children
   ___ legitimize sexual relations
   ___ companionship, especially in old age
   ___ other (specify) ______________________________

4. Why do you think fewer young professional women are marrying these days? (check as many reasons as you think appropriate)
   ___ too high standards for prospective husband
   ___ their high status intimidates men
   ___ shortage of men
   ___ they enjoy the independence living on their own affords
   ___ careers don't allow time for much personal life
   ___ they are too old
   ___ men are too demanding in what they expect women to give up for marriage
   ___ other (specify) ______________________________

5. Think for a moment about a family where both the husband and wife work at good jobs they enjoy. The wife is offered a substantial promotion in both salary and prestige. The job is in a city 100 miles away. How do you feel about her accepting the new job if:
   a) it means the couple has to live apart a few days a week? ________
   ____
   ____

   b) the husband finds a job similar to his present one at a somewhat lower salary? ______________________________
   ____
   ____

c) the wife wants to take the job but her husband doesn't particularly like it? ____________________

____

____

6. Are you currently employed? (If retired, please go to question 9.)
   ___ yes   ___ no (Go to question 11.)

7. What is your occupation? ____________________

8. How long have you worked at your present job? ____________________

9. Until you retired, what was your occupation? ____________________

10. How long did you work at the last job you held before you retired?
    ____

11. Since you first got married, have you ever worked outside the home?
    ___ yes   ___ no
    If yes, what was your occupation? ____________________

12. Did you work outside the home while your children were growing up?
    ___ yes, full time   ___ yes, part time   ___ no
    If yes:
    What was your occupation? ____________________
    Which statement comes closest to describing your feeling about working then?
    ___ I would have preferred to stay at home but my family needed the extra income.
    ___ I preferred to work and we needed the extra income.
    ___ Although we did not need the extra income, I enjoyed my job and preferred to work.

13. Do you ever envy the career and educational opportunities that are open to young women today?
    ___ yes   ___ no   ___ not sure

14. Have you ever felt that there were jobs or career opportunities that you would have liked to pursue but that were closed off to you because of your sex?
    ___ yes   ___ no
    If yes, do you think your lack of opportunities was due:
    ___ mostly to social conditions that made it hard for women to achieve
    ___ mostly to pressure from family or friends against your pursuing

opportunities
___ partly to social conditions and partly to pressure from friends or family

15. Do you feel that your daughter has more opportunities to pursue the career she wants than were open to you?
___ yes ___ no

16. In terms of your daughter's plans and aspirations for her career, please mark the spot on the scale where you see her currently (1 is lowest—achieving none of her goals yet; 7 is highest—achieving all of her goals.)
(low) 1 2 3 4 5 6 7 (high)

17. Please read each of the following statements. Which of the two comes closest to the way you feel about your daughter's goals?
___ I am supportive and proud of my daughter's ambitions and goals but I think she needs to be more realistic about what it is possible to achieve so that she will not be unhappy if things don't work out the way she planned.
___ I am supportive and proud of my daughter's ambitions and goals and try to encourage them. If things don't work out the way she planned, at least it will have been good experience for her.

18. Do you feel your daughter places her career above her personal life?
___ frequently ___ sometimes ___ never

19. Does her job allow her enough time to socialize with family and friends?
___ usually ___ occasionally ___ never

20. Recently, there has been a lot of news about women's declining chances of marriage. Do you worry about your daughter getting married?
___ frequently ___ sometimes ___ never
If you frequently or sometimes worry that she will not marry, please check any of the following statements that describe why you worry.
___ I think she would feel happier if she were married.
___ I would like grandchildren.
___ I think marriage is a better measure of success for a woman than a good career is.
___ I want to be able to tell my friends that my daughter is getting married when we are discussing our children.
___ I think her life would be more socially acceptable if she were married.

___ I think she will regret not marrying when she is older.
___ I worry about her providing for herself economically.
___ I don't want her to be lonely.
___ Other (please specify) ______________________________

Do you express your concerns to your daughter? ____________

If yes, how does she usually react? ______________________

____

____

____

21. How do you think your daughter views being unmarried?

____

____

____

____

____

____

____

22. Do you think she should be doing more to find a suitable partner?

____

____

23. Do you think she is too picky or has too high standards for the people she dates? ____

____

____

24. Do you try to introduce her to people or offer to?
___ often ___ occasionally ___ never

25. How often do you talk to your daughter about her relationships?
___ frequently ___ occasionally ___ rarely
Would you like to discuss them more than you do? ___________

26. Is your daughter seeing someone right now?
___ yes ___ no
If yes, how do you feel about the person? __________________

____

____

If no, do you feel she should be seeing someone? ___________

____

____

27. Please look at this list of qualities and check those which you would not want in someone your daughter would marry.
   ___ physically unattractive
   ___ made significantly less money than she
   ___ different religion
   ___ refused to participate in household chores
   ___ had a lower level of education than she
   ___ incapable of fathering children
   ___ insisted that she not work outside the home after marriage
   ___ sexually unfulfilling
   ___ more than 5 years younger than she
   ___ had very different political beliefs than she
   ___ strongly disliked her friends and family
   ___ less intelligent than she
   ___ other (please specify) ___________________

28. When you and your friends discuss your children, does it make you uncomfortable to say that your daughter is not married?
   ___ usually ___ sometimes ___ never

29. Think of the children of your friends and family. Would you say:
   ___ most are married
   ___ many are married but many are single
   ___ only a handful are married

30. What is your marital situation?
   ___ married
   ___ divorced
   ___ remarried
   ___ widowed

31. How long have you been married? (If divorced or widowed, how long were you married?) ___________________

32. At what age did you first marry? ___________________
   Would you say that marrying at this age was:
   ___ too young
   ___ just right
   ___ too old

33. If you had the choice to make over, would you still choose to marry your current spouse?
   ___ yes ___ no ___ not sure
   If no, why would you make a different choice? ___________

____

____

____

34. How would you categorize the options you faced for your future when you were young?
    __ I had many options, including marriage and a family which did not limit my other options in any way.
    __ I had many options but the choice of marriage and a family closed some possibilities off.
    __ My only real options were marriage and a family.
    __ Don't remember.

35. When making major decisions in your family, would you say:
    __ most decisions are made by your spouse
    __ you and your spouse share decision-making
    __ you make most of the major decisions

36. How many children do you have? ____________________

37. Can you tell us the age and marital status of all your children:
    Daughters ______________________________

    ____

    ____

    ____

    Sons ___________________________________

    ____

    ____

    ____

38. How many grandchildren do you have? ____________________

39. About which of the following subjects do you give advice to your daughter?
    __ financial matters
    __ career
    __ friends
    __ love
    __ education
    __ major purchases

40. Here is a list of qualities which parents sometimes encourage in their children. Please check the four which you think you most stressed for your daughter as she was growing up.

___ ambitious
___ popular
___ athletic
___ intelligent
___ creative
___ assertive
___ pretty
___ independent

Now we would like to know a little about your background.

41. Do you
    ___ rent apartment
    ___ own apartment
    ___ rent home
    ___ own home
    ___ other

42. What is the highest level of education you completed?
    ___ grade school
    ___ high school
    ___ some college but didn't graduate
    ___ college
    ___ postgraduate work

43. If you have completed at least some college, did you do so immediately after high school or did you go back to school later?
    ____
    ____

44. When growing up, did you live in a city with:
    ___ more than 200,000 inhabitants
    ___ between 50,000-200,000 inhabitants
    ___ between 10,000-50,000 inhabitants
    ___ less than 10,000 inhabitants

45. What is your religion?
    ___ Protestant
    ___ Catholic
    ___ Jewish
    ___ Atheist or Agnostic
    ___ Other

46. Would you say in matters of religion, you are
    ___ very religious

___ somewhat religious
___ not very religious
___ not religious at all

47. What is your current age? ______________________________

48. What is your present total family income? __________________

49. What activities and hobbies do you participate in?

____
____
____

This completes the survey. Thank you very much for your participation.

Bibliography

Aries, Philippe. *Centuries of Childhood*, trans. Robert Baldick. New York: Random House, 1962.

Austrom, Douglas and Kim Hanel. "Psychological Issues of Single Life in Canada: An Exploratory Study." *International Journal of Women's Studies*, 8, No. 1. (1985).

Becker, Gary S. *A Treatise on the Family*. Cambridge: Harvard University Press, 1981.

Bernard, Jesse. *The Future of Marriage*. New York: Bantam Books, 1973.

______________. "The Good Provider Role: Its Rise and Fall." *American Psychologist*, (1981), pp. 1-12.

Bird, Caroline. *Born Female*. New York: David McKay Co., 1968.

Blumstein, Philip and Pepper Schwartz. *American Couples*. New York: William Morrow, 1983.

Booth, Alan. "Sex and Social Participation." *American Sociological Review*, 37, No. 2. (1972).

Cherlin, Andrew. *Marriage, Divorce, Remarriage*. Boston: Harvard University Press, 1981.

______________. "Postponing Marriage: The Influence of Young Women's Work Expectations." *Journal of Marriage and the Family*, 42, No. 2 (1980), pp. 355-365.

Crone, Moira. "Rag Dolls and Difficult Mothers." *Working Mother*, May (1987), pp. 62-64.

Ehrenreich, Barbara. *The Hearts of Men: American Dreams and the Flight from Commitment*. Garden City, N.Y.: Doubleday, 1983.

Epstein, Cynthia Fuchs. *Women's Place: Options and Limits in Professional Careers*. Berkeley: University of California Press, 1970.

Friday, Nancy. *My Mother, My Self*. New York: Dell Publishing Co., 1977.

Friedman, Sonya. *Men Are Just Desserts*. New York: Warner Books, 1983.

Gagnon, John. "Success Makes You Sexy—or Does It?" *Working Mother*, April (1987), pp. 32-34.

Gerson, Kathleen. *Hard Choices: How Women Decide About Work, Career and Motherhood*. Berkeley: University of California Press, 1985.

Goldscheider, Frances Kobrin and Linda J. Waite. "Sex Differences in the Entry into Marriage." *American Journal of Sociology*, 92, No. 1 (1986).

Greenglass, Esther. "A Social-Psychological View of Marriage for Women." *International Journal of Women's Studies*, 8, No. 1 (1985).

Gross, Jane. "Single Women: Coping with a Void." *The New York Times*, April 28 (1987), p. 1.

Hewlett, Sylvia Ann. *A Lesser Life*. New York: Warner Books, 1986.

Houseknecht and Macke. "Combining Marriage and Career: The Marital Adjustment of Professional Women." *Journal of Marriage and the Family*, August (1981).

Houseknecht, Sharon K., Suzanne Vaughn and Anne Statham. "The Impact of Singlehood on the Career Patterns of Women." *Journal of Marriage and the Family*, 49, No. 2 (1987), pp. 353-366.

Huber, Joan (ed.). *Changing Women in a Changing Society*. Chicago: University of Chicago Press, 1973.

Lear, Martha Weinman. "How Many Choices Do Women *Really* Have?" *Woman's Day*, November 11 (1986).

Lenz, Elinor and Barbara Myerhoff. *The Feminization of America: How Women's Values Are Changing Our Public and Private Lives*. Los Angeles: Jeremy P. Tarcher, 1985.

Letters. "Don't Blame Single Women If the World's Changing." *The New York Times*, May 10 (1987).

Levin, John. "When Women Earn More Than Their Mates." *Working Mother*, March (1987), pp. 120-123.

Levine-Shneidman, Dr. Conalee and Karen Levine. *Too Smart For Her Own Good?*. Garden City: Doubleday, 1985.

Marini, Margaret Mooney. "The Transition to Adulthood: Sex Differences in Educational Attainment and Age at Marriage." *American Sociological Review*, 43, August (1978), pp. 483-507.

Masnick, George and Mary Jo Bane. *The Nation's Families: 1969-199O*. Boston: Auburn House Publishing Company, 1980.

Mason, Karen Oppenheim. John Czajka and Sara Arber. "Change in U.S. Women's Sex-Role Attitudes, 1964-1974." *American Sociological Review*, 41 (1976), pp. 573-592.

McBride, Angela Barron. *The Growth and Development of Mothers*. New York: Harper and Row, 1977.

Parelius, Ann P. "Emerging Sex-Role Attitudes, Expectations, and Strains Among College Women." *Journal of Marriage and the Family*, February (1975).

Regan, Mary C. and Helen E. Roland. "Rearranging Family and Career Priorities: Professional Women and Men of the Eighties." *Journal of Marriage and the Family*, November (1985).

Richardson. Laurel. *The New Other Woman: Contemporary Single Women in Affairs with Married Men*. New York: The Free Press, 1985.

Ruben, Zick, Letitia Anne Peplau and Charles T. Hill. "Loving and Leaving: Sex Differences in Romantic Attachments." *Sex Roles*, 7, No. 1 (1981), pp. 821-835.

Safilios-Rothschild, Constantina. "A Macro- and Micro-Examination of Family Power and Love: An Exchange Model." *Journal of Marriage and the Family*. May (1976), pp. 355-362.

Smith, Ralph E. (Editor) *The Subtle Revolution: Women At Work.* Washington D.C. The Urban Institute, 1979.

Spain, Daphne and Suzanne M. Bianchi. "How Women Have Changed" *American Demographics,* 1983, pp. 19-15.

Stein, Peter (Editor) *Single Life: Unmarried Adults In Social Context.* New York: St. Martin's Press, 1981.

Thorton, Arland and Deborah Freedman. *Changing Attitudes Toward Marriage and the Single Life.* Family Planning Perspectives. No. 14 (1982), pp. 297-303.

Veevers, J. E. "Voluntarily Childless Wives." *Sociology and Social Research.* 57 (1973), pp. 356-365.

Waite, Linda et al. "Non-Family Living and the Erosion of Traditional Family Orientations Among Young Adults." *American Sociological Review,* 51 (1986), pp. 541-554.

Wright, Paul H. "Men's Friendships, Women's Friendships, and the Alleged Inferiority of the Latter." *Sex Roles,* 8 (1982), pp. 1-21.